# House Cat

Revised

# How to Keep Your Indoor Cat Sane and Sound

## Christine Church

**Howell**
Book House™

Howell Book House

Published by Wiley Publishing, Inc., Hoboken, New Jersey

For general information on our other products and services or to obtain technical support please contact our Customer Care Department within the U.S. at (800) 762-2974, outside the U.S. at (317) 572-3993 or fax (317) 572-4002.

Wiley also publishes its books in a variety of electronic formats. Some content that appears in print may not be available in electronic books. For more information about Wiley products, please visit our web site at www.wiley.com.

Library of Congress Cataloging-in-Publication Data:

Church, Christine.

House Cat : how to keep your indoor cat sane and sound / Christine Church.— Rev.

p. cm.

Includes index.

ISBN 0-7645-7741-7 (pbk.)

1. Cats. I. Title.

SF447.C5 2004

636.8—dc22

2004023104

Printed in the United States of America

10  9  8  7  6  5  4  3  2  1

Revised Edition

Book design by LeAndra Hosier

All photos by Christine Church, except where noted.

Book production by Wiley Publishing, Inc. Composition Services

# Dedication

For Taffy, whose life brought sunshine to mine and all who knew her. I am glad I was able to give you sunshine in the end. August 1983–September 2001

For Teisha, who, despite her blindness, could see very clearly into my heart for the ten years she was with me. ??–February 2002

For Candy, thank you for two decades of love and holding your large double paw in my hand at night when I was alone. September 1983–August 2003

And, to Gillie, always the trooper, who battled cancer with a spirit like none other. A true inspiration, you learned to walk on three legs as if you were born to it and you never let illness bring you down. Always happy, always loving. You greeted every stranger with purrs and head-butts and brought smiles to all who met you. I miss how you would grab my manuscript pages as I worked and try to run off with them. You were gone from my life far too soon. June 20, 1992–February 18, 2004

A very special dedication to New England Veterinary Oncology Group (NEVOG), who cared for Gillie with gentle hands and gentle hearts. To Dr. Kim L.Cronin, DVM, DACVIM (oncology), a fantastic vet and wonderful person. And to the receptionists (Sandi, thank you for the laughs) and to the techs. You treated and saw Gillie as one of the family, letting him hop around behind the reception desk, always greeting him with big smiles and lots of treats. It made his experience (and the long drive for my brother and me) so much more bearable. I will never forget you. You gave Gillie life, until he chose his own time to move on. Thank you!

And to my brother, Correy, for taking the time to bring Gillie and me to each appointment. Thank you!

*Gillie, June 1992–February 2004*

# Contents

## 9
## The Lost Cat, 197

## 10
## Cats in the Kitchen, 207

## 11
## The Aging Cat, 219

# Preface

L oved and worshipped, hated and feared, cats have been companions to humanity for thousands of years.

A carnivorous mammal in the *Felidae* family, the cat's evolutionary origin is not a clear picture. The most ancient known ancestor is an animal called Miacis, which had a slender body and short legs. As for our own dear *Felis domesticus*, fossils resembling the modern domestic cat, a cross between *Felis sylvestris* and *Felis lybica*, date back some ten to twelve million years.

The earliest known companion cat dates to about 4,500 years ago, when a cat was buried with its master in an Egyptian tomb. Called *mau*, resembling the sound cats make (the word also means "to see"), cats in Egypt were often mummified and placed in tombs as members of the family. Sometimes mummified mice were placed in the tombs with the cats to ensure their sustenance in the afterlife. In 1890, at one ancient tomb complex in Egypt, 300,000 cat mummies were discovered.

Cats were considered sacred to the Egyptians, who were grateful to them for ridding the granaries of mice. They showed their appreciation by deifying their feline helpers in the persona of a half cat, half woman goddess named Bast.

By the beginning of the Middle Ages in Europe, cats were still tolerated as mouse-catching aids, but by the middle of the thirteenth century things began to change. Many beliefs and practices of the old pagan religions still existed at the time, and these beliefs came under intense persecution. Because the rites of the pagan goddess of fertility, Freya, include a role for the cat, cats too were accused and persecuted. The animals were seen as carriers of evil, brought about by their mysterious nature. Witches also came to be associated with cats. This belief led to authorized persecution of cats, and by the year 1400 cats were close to extinction.

This attitude nearly led to the extinction of people, as well, as ships bringing the Crusaders home also brought rats carrying the plague to Europe. The Black Death spread across the continent, and two-thirds of the population was exterminated because there were not enough cats left to rid the towns of the deadly rodents.

Cat populations revived after the plague, but cats did not regain the respect and admiration once accorded them by the Egyptians until the mid-1800s, when scientists were able to conclusively prove that bacteria and germs cause illness, not evil spirits or witches. Cats were once again seen in their true light as the epitome of cleanliness.

By the seventeenth century cats had arrived in America, brought on ships as rat catchers. They were quickly put to work in the New World earning their keep on farms and eventually found their way back into the hearts of most—loved and honored once more.

Today, there are more than fifty-five million cat owners in the United States, making cats the number-one household pet. Like the Egyptians before them, many people who own cats treat them with the same respect as any other loved member of the family. Their place of honor and affection in society seems secure.

# Acknowledgments

**M**any thanks go to my special friend and editor Beth Adelman, for without her guidance this book would not have been. And to Kathy Nebenhaus for making it all possible. And thank you to Ria Brown for her assistance.

Also, a thanks goes out to Bolton Veterinary Hospital for answering my questions so patiently each time I called.

I would also like to thank the following:

Dr. Cassandra Oswald for her care and help.

Dr. Zyra, DVM, for recommending NEVOG.

To my wonderful cats, Sammy, Shadow, Pounce, and Mikai, for always knowing when I am ill emotionally or physically. And for putting aside your desires to sleep in your usual locations and instead remaining with me, keeping me warm and comforted, the entire night after Gillie was lost to us. And Wolfe, my special Doberman, who slept at bedside.

Thanks, too, to my black rat Ben, for helping me write this book by pitter-pattering across the keyboard, believing you know more about cats than I do. And, of course I can't leave out the other members of the rat gang: Liam, Hairy Potter, Viktor, Isabeau, Marishka, Methos, Aleera, and Mina.

And though he had no part in the writing of this book, I have to acknowledge my horse, Kobeejo, for his beauty, love, and dedication.

# Introduction

I would like to tell you a true story. I am not relaying this story to illustrate why indoor cats live better, longer lives. No, the moral to this story is something completely different.

Gillie was an outdoor cat almost all his life. He was smart and extremely friendly to people. As a matter of fact, one could say he literally craved attention and petting and never gave up the opportunity to get them. During the day his favorite activity was sleeping in the sunshine near the house where he lived.

I knew Gillie. He lived less than a block away and was acquired as an adorable black-and-white kitten, complete with a "goatee," by my best friend's mother, Jane, in 1992.

However, in 1998 Jane passed away and my friend Kris inherited Gillie. Being mostly an outdoor cat, he seemed to require little: food placed out for him twice a day, a warm basement to sleep in on cold nights, and as much petting as he could embezzle. Other than the occasional battering from neighborhood cats (his apparent motto was "I'm a lover, not a fighter," proven by the notches and scars that were the distinctive features of his ears), being outdoors seemed to suit Gillie fine. Besides, one glimpse at Kris's large fostered Shepherd guide dogs and Gillie would bolt in the other direction.

Gillie was a special cat in my life, even then. I cared for him when my friend vacationed, and he would often appear from the bushes for pets and kisses when I visited. I clearly remember one particular vacation when Gillie was in my care, and together we sat on the stairs in the living room, watching out the front door as a storm rolled in from the south. He sat regally at my side, purring loudly in contentment over the growing sounds of thunder as I petted him.

Kris and I discussed the possibility of Gillie becoming my cat, though I wondered, at his age (he was 10 years old) how well he would acclimate not only to my cats, but to life indoors. He was doing just fine right where he was.

Not two weeks after this conversation, Kris noticed a lump on Gillie's hind leg. It had grown quickly, seemingly overnight. And when Gillie was brought in to the veterinarian's, the news was grim. Gillie had cancer.

The tumor seemed localized, and hopes were high that it would be removed without consequence, that it had not spread. But, as unpredictable as life can be at times, several hours into the day Kris received a phone call. Gillie's leg would have to be amputated, right up to his hip. The cancer had spread beyond the tumor alone. It was an injection-related fibrosarcoma, a rare but unfortunate side effect from the feline leukemia vaccinations he'd received annually, to keep him safe from developing the disease from an infected cat he might encounter outside.

Distraught and in tears, Kris called me. She could not care for Gillie with the large dogs that lived in her house. He would have to be put to sleep, or I could take him, as we had discussed only weeks earlier. Of course, the choice was simple.

I picked Gillie up when he was ready and brought him to his new home. For the weeks of his recovery he was kept in a large dog crate, padded for comfort and furnished with a low-sided litter box as he got used to life on three legs, as well as food, water, toys, and a catnip-filled bed to rub and sleep on. He was also kept in a room closed off from the other cats.

By the time Gillie had healed about a month or so later, and was finally, slowly allowed to roam the house with the other cats, I was actually surprised at the simplicity of the introductions. Gillie had picked up the scents of the home, and the other cats had grown accustomed to his. He easily became one of the family.

Life as a strictly indoor cat seemed to be natural for Gillie. He liked to sit by the window and watch the world outside or simply soak up the sunshine, yet he never seemed to long for the outdoors. He had all he needed: attention, petting, and love whenever he desired it (and desire it he did); food always available when he craved it; several cat trees of wood and carpet and sisal rope to jump onto and dig his claws into; and even other cats to keep company with. Cats who did not attack him or try to add to the notches in his ears, but rather two friends in particular who would often bathe him as he lounged on my bed. And he discovered something he truly loved: toy jingle balls. He never seemed to tire of the concept that batting those balls with a paw would make them roll away so he could catch them, again and again.

Unfortunately, this new life was all too short, for Gillie's cancer returned. It had spread beyond the leg and into the area of his spine and hips. And so, northward we traveled, an hour and a half away, to the New England Veterinary Oncology Group, and for over a year Gillie received palliative treatments. The cancer was too aggressive, had spread too far, to be cured, and I thought often of what I would do the day I knew the treatments would no longer work. But the treatments did work, every time. And though the cancer always returned as expected, each treatment would shrink it away again. Through it all, Gillie never faltered in his loving, friendly, and play-ful nature. He never crammed himself, frightened, in the back of the carrier, refusing to come out. Instead, Gillie would be waiting at the carrier door, meowing for it to be opened, so he could receive pets, kisses, and treats from the receptionists, and even to hop about behind the counter.

It was a chilly February night, 2004. Gillie was playing with one of his jingle balls. He had been in for a treatment the week before and, as usual, was doing well. Later that night I saw him asleep curled comfortably in a cat bed beneath the back room desk. He liked the cat beds because I placed the same catnip sleep sacks in them that he would sleep on in the crate when he had first arrived here after the surgery to remove his back leg.

The next morning, he did not come for breakfast. Usually he was the first cat to the food bowls. I felt something was terribly wrong. I went to the desk and saw he was still curled in the cat bed just as he had been the night before. Deep inside I knew he was gone, but part of me still hoped he was only sleeping soundly and when I touched him, he would look at me sleepily and yawn. It took me a few moments as I stood there to compose myself, before I knelt down and reached to him, confirming my deepest fear.

He had died peacefully, in his sleep, on one of the catnip beds he loved. I never had to make the decision or worry about the day the cancer would make him too ill to go on. An underlying heart condition or an aneurysm or some other undetectable infirmity had made the decision for me.

As you might think about a book outlining the hows and whys of keeping cats indoors twenty-four hours a day, this story was not meant to illustrate why cats should be kept inside, but rather to point out that even a cat who is happy and healthy living out of doors might someday need to be brought inside permanently. It also illustrates that not all outdoor cats will resent or even argue with their new indoor life, if they are trained and acclimated properly. Chapter 1 will list many reasons to keep or bring your cat indoors, and will also discuss cats who have lived long and fruitful lives out of doors, what the difference is, and why.

As you read through these chapters, true and rhetorical stories will illustrate many of the points so you can understand how to use the advice and knowledge in your own and your cat's life.

A cat's basic needs remain the same, indoors or out, and the key to keeping them happy indoors is still to appease their natural desires. However, since the publication of the original *Housecat* in 1998, many things have changed in the world of indoor cats as more and more people realize the benefits of bringing their cats in, or never letting them out. New foods and litters made specially for house cats are only one of the many examples of these changes. As time goes on, many things grow, shift, and alter. The world of the cat is no different. It is up to us, as our cats' caretakers, to understand and keep up with these changes.

# 1

# Safety in the Eyes of the Cat

She eyes the bird with sharp vision. The robin's movement as it tugs a worm from the earth is too enticing to ignore. Her body lowers, her ears perk forward, though she's unaware of it. Instinct drives her now as she slinks slowly onward, her belly almost dragging on the lush, green grass. She is not hungry, for those who care for her feed her well, yet still this desire moves her forward, slowly so as not to frighten the bird into flight before she can reach it. Precise timing is imperative: If she bolts too soon the bird will take flight; too late and she might not be able to stop in time for the catch. These thoughts don't run consciously through her mind, only through her blood and adrenaline. She does not know why she does this, only that the desire is strong, it is everything, it is her entire focus. The world around her has disappeared. All that matters is the bird.

She is now within striking distance. She takes off, ready, all her focus sharp on the robin. She is not aware of the car coming quickly toward her until the squealing of the brakes snaps her concentration and sends the robin soaring away into the sky. Confusion ensues and she's not sure what to do, but it doesn't matter. There's no avoiding the large tires heading straight for her.

## Understanding Danger

As time moves along and cats become increasingly integrated into our society and families, more and more people are keeping their precious felines strictly indoors. Yet many still believe cats are aloof and free-natured and need to be allowed their "freedom."

As the story above details, cats do indeed possess many of the instincts passed to them through thousands of years of feline heritage. They still love the chase and the catch. Instincts can also lead them to shelter when the weather is poor or to water when they are thirsty, and often, with very advanced olfactory nerves, to food when they need it. Yet most of these are basic instincts just about every animal possesses, whether wild or domesticated. Even humans possess them to some degree.

But those very instincts that were meant to save and aid cats in the wild can prove deadly under certain circumstances. The cats who evolved into our domesticated feline did not have cars to contend with or antifreeze left on driveways that can poison them. Their instincts help them avoid natural dangers, not the ones we make, and despite their seemingly aloof nature, most cats in the wild do not live alone. Even feral cats live in colonies; there's safety in numbers and cats instinctively know this.

However, when you let Puss out to go and roam the neighborhood, she is alone. Other cats who were not raised in her territory are seen as a threat. Fights can cause terrible wounds and infection. Most cats have little or no awareness of the peril of a moving vehicle. And though cars are the most common reason outdoor cats lose their lives, other dangers exist as well. Even in rural areas where there are few cars, potential peril dwells.

At one time it was unheard of to even so much as mention keeping a cat strictly indoors. People mumbled that it was cruel or inhumane to keep an animal with such a wild nature "locked away."

Fortunately, this outlook is waning in popularity. According to a 1996 national survey by the American Pet Products Manufacturers Association, two-thirds of all cat owners keep their cats indoors all the time. The number of cats kept exclusively indoors has grown throughout the years, and as the population rises and lifestyles become faster, this number should continue to rise.

But are cats happy staying indoors? That is the question posed most often. And the answer is that it depends on the cat and her circumstance and surroundings, as well as other factors such as her upbringing, personality, and acclimation to the world within walls.

I won't lie to you. I have seen cats whose lives benefit from living outdoors. For example, Yappy is a beautiful tabby-and-white cat who lives at the stable where I board my horse. The stable is well off the street, and hundreds of acres of land surround it. Yet Yappy rarely strays far from the barn. He has learned to avoid horses' hooves (just as, yes, some cats do learn to avoid cars) and he loves all the people and attention he receives. He reminds me quite a bit of Gillie, whose story I told in the Introduction of this book. Yappy spends most of his time sleeping on hay bales inside the indoor riding ring, but he also craves attention. Anyone who sits to watch the riders invariably finds Yappy in their lap, purring and kneading. With all that land and freedom, he prefers indoors, the people, and particularly, the laps. But cats who live with such freedom and remain safe are the exception rather than the rule.

There's a wide misconception that keeping a cat inside is ludicrous, even cruel. This belief leads to the notion that the quality of an indoor cat's life is diminished. But the truth is that if a cat is raised in a proper indoor environment, she can very well enjoy both quality and quantity of life.

A comfortable indoor environment can be created for just about any cat. There is little the outdoors has to offer a cat that cannot be satisfactorily simulated indoors. Sunshine can be brought in through windows, window perches, and outdoor enclosures (see chapter 7). Cats can be just as happy chasing catnip mice and interactive cat toys as they can real mice and birds (and they cannot contract parasites and diseases from toys). Cat trees are just as satisfying to a cat as real trees, and cats don't need the kind of room to run that dogs do. Being short-distance sprinters by design, cats get plenty of exercise running from room to room.

The notion that an indoor cat is "locked up," as if the animal were kept in a prison, is completely false. The cat does not see it this way, particularly a cat who has been raised indoors her entire life. The

*Napping on a pillow is far more comfortable than napping on the pavement.*

belief that an indoor cat "suffers" likens the complexity of a cat's mind to the complexity of a human's—and it's not an accurate comparison. Watch your indoor cat gazing outside at the birds and squirrels, tail flicking, eyes wide. It may seem as if the cat is frustrated at not being allowed out. But to the cat, the window is like a television screen where she can sit and watch a fascinating "movie."

Cats spend three-quarters of their lives asleep, and often owners of outdoor cats confuse the contentment of an indoor cat's slumber with boredom. Because they do not see their outdoor cat's activities as often, they do not realize their outdoor cat is most likely curled up under a tree somewhere, taking the same catnap she would if she were indoors.

Our cats are no longer wild animals. Humans domesticated cats thousands of years ago. Despite their independence, cats need humans to protect them from dangers. Most of these dangers were created by humans, and now that cats live with us in our world, it's our responsibility to see to their safety.

## Outdoor Dangers

A cat's ability to reason and protect herself in the outdoors is not much more complex than that of a 2- or 3-year-old child's. They know enough to be fearful of certain circumstances, but do not always know where to look or what to do.

## Bringing Kitty In

Shelter workers and those individuals who handle and work with stray, abandoned, and ill cats know firsthand the dangers that face an outdoor cat. Most breeders and shelters allow their cats to leave their facility only under the strict condition that the cat remains indoors. Even adoption centers are requiring adopters to keep their cats strictly indoors.

Of course, there are indoor dangers that may befall cats, but those are, for the most part, controllable. As soon as your cat walks out the door, she is no longer under your supervision and is exposed to any danger that may await. The choice, ultimately, is up to you, but consider these dangers that are faced by cats that roam outdoors.

## Cars

The number-one cause of death and injury to cats allowed outside is cars. Think of everyone you know whose cats are allowed free access to the outdoors and, chances are, at least one of them will have had the horrifying experience of losing a cat, or at least of their cat being injured by a car. If all those people had simply not allowed their cats to roam, they would have been spared that particular agony.

But being hit by a car is not the only car-related threat posed to a free-roaming cat. Cats love warmth, and there's no better place to find it on a cold winter's night than under the hood of a warmed engine. If the car is started while the cat is curled up inside, the cat could very well be maimed or killed. I will never forget the Buick I owned about fifteen years ago. One day the car was running poorly, so my father, a mechanic, checked under the hood. To my horror he found the long-dead carcass of a kitten securely attached to the engine. It had been there since before I bought the car.

Other potential dangers can come from inside the car. An open window can be a great enticement to an outdoor cat. Midnight, an outdoor cat from birth, was extremely fond of the comforts found inside a car. She had been inadvertently taken on many trips by climbing into an open car window and curling up in the back seat. One time she disappeared after taking an unplanned trip to work with her caretaker. Midnight had curled up in the back of his pickup truck, and he drove off unaware that she was there. When he arrived at work, the cat jumped out and disappeared into the woods behind the building. Fortunately, she was recovered four days later.

That trip could have been fatal to Midnight. She could have leaped from the back of the truck while it moved along on the highway or been hit by a car in the unfamiliar area where she hid those four days until she was enticed out with food and caught.

Riding loose in a car, to the vet or wherever you might be bringing your cat, is another danger I have heard stories about all too often. The cat can get under your feet, causing an accident, or out an open window. In the summer, the temperature inside a car can reach deadly highs, even in the shade—which is why you should never leave a cat in a parked car in the heat, not even for a moment.

## Falls

When people think of a cat falling, they always picture the graceful feline landing gently on her feet. But the reality is that many cats have died from falling off fences, balconies, roofs, and even out of trees. The most common injury to cats who have fallen is a split palate. What surprises most people is that cats are often injured worse from shorter falls than longer ones. This is because of the way the cat twists her body as she falls and readies herself to land. A shorter distances leaves less time for the motions necessary to land with no or minimal injury.

## Diseases

There are many diseases cats can contract from other cats or wild animals (see chapter 8), most of which can be fatal to your cat. Some of these include rabies, toxoplasmosis, feline infectious peritonitis (FIP), feline leukemia virus (FeLV), feline immunodeficiency virus (FIV), and feline t-lymphocytic virus (FTLV or Feline AIDS). Some of these diseases, such as rabies and toxoplasmosis, may also be passed from your cat to you. Although vaccinations are available for rabies, FeLV, and now FIP (an intranasal vaccine), they are not always a 100-percent guarantee that your cat will not contract these illnesses. And for other illnesses there are no vaccines. Some vaccinations, as Gillie's story in the introduction illustrates, may also cause vaccination-site fibrosarcoma—a rare form of cancer. This problem is currently being researched, but is still an issue. Whether or not your indoor cat needs some or any of these vaccines will be discussed in chapter 8.

## Parasites

Parasites may be a problem for any cat, indoors or out, but free-roaming cats have a much higher risk of picking up fleas, ticks, worms, lice, and mites than cats who are kept indoors. Parasites may also be contracted if your cat eats a rodent or wild animal, which is less likely if your cat is kept strictly indoors.

In addition to the damage parasites do all by themselves, they carry many serious diseases. For example, any cat with access to wooded areas may pick up ticks infected with Lyme disease, particularly in the northeastern region of the United States. If not caught and treated early, Lyme disease may cause serious health problems for your cat, and for you. Parasites can also cause worms, which feed on the nutrients that enter the cat's digestive tract, causing the cat to slowly starve.

## Other Animals

Cats allowed outdoors are subject to the attacks of wild animals, venomous snakes, insects, dogs, and other cats. Wild animals, often forced from their homes due to building projects, are increasingly stealing household pets for food. Coyotes have been known to easily carry off cats. Eagles do not know the difference between your kitten and a rabbit to feed their young hatchlings. Do you live in an area

*A cat outside is at ten times the risk of death
or injury than an indoor cat.*

with rattlesnakes, scorpions, poisonous spiders? You cannot watch your cat when she is outdoors to keep her safe from these threats.

## Humans

Humans can be another source of danger for cats allowed to roam free. As much as we love our cats, there are people who don't share the same feelings, and cats allowed outdoors are subject to dangerously cruel pranks.

Cats might also get into a neighbor's garbage, which could be dangerous to the cat if she swallows bones or a poisonous substance such as a cleaning chemical. Bad relations and squabbles between neighbors can be born from a cat howling at night, tearing apart garbage bags, planting muddy paws all over a precious car, spraying urine on prize roses, digging up vegetation, or any other instinctive yet destructive acts.

Not long ago, the Humane Society Adoption Center had a cat in its care, and the card on the animal's cage, which gives the cat's information and why it was given up, stated: "Reason for surrender: Accused of scratching neighbor's car." There have been many lawsuits brought against people whose cats have destroyed property and livestock. Even in the country, cats are at tremendous risk when allowed outside.

## Poisons

Cats allowed outdoors can crawl under cars and may get oil, gasoline, or antifreeze on their coats. As they clean their coats, the toxins enter their bloodstream. Antifreeze is particularly dangerous to your cat, since it has a sweet taste and cats may lick it from a driveway or their paws.

Pesticides or chemical treatments on lawns and gardens can also poison your cat, if she walks on a treated lawn and then lick her paws.

## Hunting, Trapping, and Fishing

Bajor was a beautiful shorthaired black-and-white feral cat who lived his life in comfort at Kitty Angels Humane Society in Coventry, Connecticut. But this was not always the case. Caught in a leg-hold trap before being found and brought to the shelter, Bajor had lost a leg.

Areas with hunting and trapping seasons are dangerous to free-roaming cats, because they are no better than a wild animal at seeing where a trap is set. Many cats have been killed or have lost limbs after being caught in leg-hold traps. A cat may also be mistaken for a game animal and shot.

Areas where fishing is a prevalent sport or business can hold dangers for cats as well. Cats can become tangled in fishing lines or be injured by a hook.

## Getting Lost

As keen as are cats' senses and abilities to find their way, they may still get lost, particularly if you have just moved to a new area or if the weather is bad and the cat gets disoriented (see chapter 9 for what to do if your cat gets lost). Unlike dogs, lost cats are not usually recovered. In areas where there are no leash or licensing laws for cats, free-roaming cats are not often picked up by shelter wardens and taken back to the shelter, where their owners can easily find them. And people who see unfamiliar cats roaming may not be as quick to take them in and search for their owners, simply assuming they are "outdoor" cats.

## Overpopulation

The overpopulation of cats is a major concern. Millions of cats each year are put to death just because there are not enough homes for them

all. If your cat is unaltered (not spayed or neutered) and is allowed to run free, chances are good that you're adding to the numbers. Even if you find a "good home" for all your female cat's kittens, you really can't be sure those kittens are not going to produce more kittens who will end up in a shelter or in the street—unless you know for a fact that they are all altered and remain with their families for their entire lives. I've heard people say, "I did my part and found good homes; it's not my problem." Actually, it is. It's everyone's problem. The cats or kittens killed in a shelter or starving on the street could have been spared if everyone's pet cats were altered.

## Weather and Natural Disasters

Severe fires have struck Southern California, Colorado, and other parts of the United States, ravaging neighborhoods and destroying thousands of homes. In some cases, people were evacuated so quickly they had little time to pack or think of what to take with them. Many cats were lost, killed, maimed, and injured, particularly outdoor cats whose owners could not find them when it was time to leave.

In severe weather, cats tend to hide and to become disoriented or lost. If a natural disaster such as a hurricane, flood, tornado, earthquake, fire, or mudslide strikes your area, it is much more difficult to find a free-roaming cat in the event of evacuation or finding shelter. An outdoor cat may disappear and later return home to find no one there, or worse, no home there. She may get hurt or lost in her attempt to find food, shelter, water, or her owners (see chapter 9 for what to do in an emergency). Even a cat hiding from a severe thunderstorm can get hurt, disoriented, or lost.

## Sickness

If your cat develops a medical problem, symptoms are much easier to notice if your cat is home all the time. It may be difficult to detect

---

### For Your Cat's Safety

Unaltered cats, male and female, are at a much higher risk of injury and danger, as they tend to roam farther and more frequently than altered cats. It is just as important to have your male cat altered as it is your female. Males are extremely relentless in their search for a mate and will continue to add to the overpopulation problem throughout their entire lives.

Even indoor-only cats should be altered, as they may get out accidentally. In addition, a female in heat will drive you crazy with her caterwauling and attempts to get out to find a mate. A male cat may spray a foul-smelling urine all over your house, and this odor is almost impossible to remove, particularly from carpets and upholstery.

the early signs of an illness in a cat who is outdoors most or all of the time. With certain conditions, early diagnosis is essential to successful treatment, so your outdoor cat's health is at risk that way, too.

## More Points to Ponder

In addition to the specific dangers lurking outdoors, there are other factors to consider when you weigh the merits of an indoor life for your cat.

Even if an outdoor cat manages to escape falling victim to one or more of the tragedies I've just described, life for the average outdoor cat, even that of a pampered pet, is much more stressful than the indoor-only lifestyle. Cats on the street, or even in the country, are faced every day with territorial disputes and threats from other animals, cats, and even people. Outdoors, cats must learn to sleep with one eye open, so to speak, to protect themselves from dangers that may creep up on them in their slumber. Indoor cats, however, are usually the epitome of relaxation.

### Better Pets

Just tonight I was in the grocery store browsing through the cat food aisle. Two women walked past me, talking about a cat. "Does your cat come in much?" one of the women asked. "No," the other replied, "he stays out most of the time now that the weather is warmer."

Indoor cats generally make much better pets than cats allowed outdoors whenever they wish. Since indoor cats are in your company most or all the time when you are home, you can both appreciate each other's company a lot more.

Cats can be wonderful animals to observe, and what better place to observe their playful leaps and chases than in the comfort of home? Also, because they do not have the distraction of wanting to go out all the time, indoor cats turn their attention to loving their owners instead of the neighborhood. A domestic cat is a companion animal, and she should be allowed to be just that—a companion.

## Longer Life Span

The average life span of an outdoor cat is three to five years, while the average life span of a cat kept strictly indoors is between fourteen and twenty years. This age has risen in recent years. This is due not only to the lack of danger, but also to the advancement of veterinary care. Studies have shown that outdoor cats, on average, do not receive the same medical attention as indoor cats.

*Candy lived to be 20 years old as an indoor cat.*

## A Healthy Coat

It's only when I pet an outdoor cat that I realize just how much cleaner and softer my indoor cats are. Not only do indoor cats have a lower incidence of parasites, but unless they develop an illness or allergy, their coats are healthier overall as well. Indoor cats rarely get into anything that soils their coats. They're not exposed to the smog and pollution outdoor cats are exposed to, either, and it usually shows in their fur with a healthy, luxurious sheen.

## Environmental Issues

I will never forget the time I was watching a bright red cardinal feeding in our yard when suddenly, seemingly from out of nowhere, the neighbor's cat leaped into the tree and captured the bird before it had a chance to fly away. The cat ran away, the frightened bird screeching loudly from within her jaws.

Many people enjoy watching wildlife, and particularly birds. They embellish their lawns with bird feeders and baths to attract these winged wonders in all their glorious beauty. These people may not appreciate the natural instincts a cat has to chase and kill birds, thus hindering bird-watching for the whole neighborhood. As author Cleveland Amory said in his book *The Cat Who Came for Christmas*, "I feel that no cat owner has the right to jeopardize the right of his neighbor who may enjoy his birds just as the cat owner enjoys his cat."

Roaming cats may also kill endangered species of birds and wildlife. While our pets are descended from predators, the cats who live in our homes are domesticated animals, meaning their numbers are not limited in a natural way, as with wild species. It is up to us, as those who domesticated cats, to make sure our pets do not upset nature's delicate balance by allowing our cats to roam and kill.

## Legal Issues

In some areas leash laws exist not only for dogs, but for cats as well. These laws vary from community to community, and the term "leash law" means different things, depending on the law. For example, some ordinances say a cat must be confined to the owner's premises, and others say cats must be kept leashed or caged when out of the house. Bowling Green, Ohio, enacted a cat confinement law in 1984. According to this law, cats should be confined to the owner's property or under the owner's physical control at all times. Also, cats who are leash-trained are not to be walked on a leash longer than 10 feet.

These laws are created as a service not only to the cat and cat owner, but as a courtesy to the public. Free-roaming cats can be an annoyance to neighbors, destroying property and trespassing in areas where they are not wanted, and they can become injured.

Rabies is another issue that has recently been addressed by many laws. In areas with a high incidence of rabies, laws requiring that all cats have vaccines are common. In Connecticut, if a cat is picked up outdoors and the owner cannot furnish proof that the cat has been vaccinated for rabies, a fine is imposed.

## Making the Decision

Many cats who have spent a good deal of their time outdoors, such as strays and barn cats, may seem as if they simply cannot adjust to life indoors. They can become lonely, bored, and destructive. For someone who is unaccustomed to training a cat to stay indoors or someone who is gone most of the time, this task may seem nearly impossible. These cat owners may become frustrated and feel that although the cat's life may be shortened, the cat will be happier in the long run being allowed outside. However, with patience and proper strategy, almost any cat, no matter how accustomed to the outdoor life, can be acclimated to a life indoors (see chapter 2).

Of course, there are exceptions to every rule, and at times, no matter what the owner does, the cat just insists on having things her own way. I have known of such cats—but very few—and feel, in many of the cases, that the owners did not try hard enough and gave up too soon.

My cat Taffy (who passed away in September 2001) always longed for the outdoors, eyeing the door but respecting the fact that she was not able to go out. About a year before she passed away, I was able to grant her wish. Arthritic and going blind, she could safely wander my large fenced yard and the garden at last. She could not get under the fence, and her frailty kept her from climbing over. She never showed any desire to leave that yard. Her favorite place was the garden on a nice sunny day, and I am grateful I was able to give her that in her golden years.

*Fencing and other enclosures enable even indoor
cats to enjoy the sunshine outside.*

The most effective way of providing your cat with an appropriately appealing indoor environment is to know what your cat, and all cats, would enjoy in an outdoor setting. Cats, by instinct, have certain needs and desires, such as scratching, marking territorial boundaries, eating grass, chasing prey, and playing. By providing your cat with the proper equipment, toys, space, attention, and love (all of which will be discussed in this book), your cat will have at her disposal a complete environment—indoors.

The decision to keep your cat indoors is yours. But remember that owning a cat is a privilege that should not be taken lightly. A cat is not a toy; she is a living animal with feelings and needs. All cats, even ones who spend time outdoors, need and enjoy affection and playtime with their owners. They benefit from interaction, and it will benefit you as well. Cats are wonderful stress reducers, and that's been proven scientifically.

As you read this book, you will have a better perspective of what it will take to keep your indoor cat happy and make your feline friend the ultimate companion. And you will discover that an indoor cat, if given the proper environment, can truly be a happy cat.

# 2

# Important Introductions

The kitten did not know where he was going. All he knew was that one moment he was warm and cuddled with his mother and siblings, and the next he was in a dark box, moving, being taken away. He remembered there were people there, confusion, but it all happened so fast. And now he was in the dark, bumping about with no knowledge of where he was being taken, or why. There were small holes, but he could not see well out of them, so he sat back, trying to hide in one corner, and cried for his mother. Every now and again he would see a human eye peer through one of the holes and voices would speak, but he did not recognize any of them.

And then at last the moving ended and the box was open. Bright light swarmed in, and he squinted but did not move. He was curious as to what could be out there, yet frightened as well. However, the choice was made for him as large hands reached in and scooped him up. He was placed on the floor. Nothing smelled or looked familiar. He looked up at the people standing around him as if waiting for him to do something.

He felt a need to relieve himself; being so overwhelmed, he had not realized it until now and so he searched, cautiously for a place to go.

The people followed, watching. This made him even more nervous. They were watching him and making all that noise, saying, "Come here, Kitty" and "Don't go over there, Kitty," but he did not understand a word of it.

He could not hold it any longer. He found a nice soft place, dug a bit, and relieved himself. But much screaming ensued and he was snatched up. The woman screamed, "My Persian carpet! I told you we should have bought the litter box first!"

## Before Bringing Your New Cat Home

Remember how it feels to tear open a birthday gift to find out what's inside? That same excitement awaits the person who is ready to bring

*Every cat should have one dish he can call his own.*

home a new cat or kitten. Regardless of whether he is your first or your thirtieth cat, the anticipation is still there. But it is important to remember, for your new cat's sake as well as your own, that certain provisions should be made before your kitten or cat's arrival. For people already blessed with one or more cats at home, this should be simple, as almost everything needed should already be on hand. But there are still preparations to be made, and the following should always be ready for your new pet:

- Litter box and litter (see chapter 4 for the scoop on litter and boxes)
- Food and water dishes (see chapter 10 for more information on your indoor cat's nutritional needs)
- Scratching post or tree (see chapter 5 for advice on choosing the best one)
- Cat carrier, for safe trips to the vet or groomer; the carrier you choose should be of sturdy plastic, rather than the cardboard type, as some cats hate the confinement of a carrier so much they will actually try their hardest to break out of it (see Carrier Training later in this chapter for how to acclimate your cat to riding in a carrier)
- Grooming tools (see chapter 6 for grooming and bathing tips)
- Toys (if you're not convinced that toys are vital to a cat's health, see chapter 3)

## Vet Check

Always bring any new cat or kitten to the veterinarian for a checkup and to be tested for feline leukemia virus, feline infectious peritonitis, and feline AIDS before bringing him into your home, especially if you have other cats. Make an appointment to stop by the vet's office right after picking up your new cat.

# Cat-Proofing

Although your indoor cat will not be faced with cars, wild animals, or any of the other dangers posed outdoors, many hidden dangers can lurk in unexpected locations, especially for a young kitten who is rambunctious and full of mischief. Kittens seem to have the remarkable ability to find trouble in the most innocuous places. But, unlike outdoor dangers, most household dangers are controllable, and cat-proofing your house before you bring your new cat home can help prevent accidents.

Look around your house carefully and remove anything that may spell danger to your new pet. Use common sense and imagination; try to think like a cat when determining what trouble your new cat can get into as you move from room to room. Get down on your hands and knees and look around. Then remember that cats can jump and climb to high places, too.

## The Kitchen

The best place to start is the kitchen. Chemicals, household cleaners, detergents, paint, dye, antifreeze, mothballs, bleach, rat poisons, and insecticides may all be harmful to a curious kitty. Kittens, in particular, love to eat the inedible, so anything of potential harm should be kept in an unbreakable container and secured tightly in a closet or cupboard.

Anything small enough to fit into a kitten's mouth (such as milk jug rings or twist ties) should be kept out of your pet's reach at all times.

The stove can be quite hazardous if cooking food is left unattended with a rambunctious cat or kitten around. After cooking, wait until the burners have cooled before allowing your cat access to the kitchen.

The refrigerator is another potential hazard area that should be watched closely. Cats soon learn that food is kept in that big box, and some love to climb inside and see what they can nibble on. As a kitten, my cat Shadow took unending delight in climbing into the refrigerator every time it was opened. Fortunately, he was always spotted and removed before the door was closed, but such has not always been the case with other cats. Cats have frozen or suffocated to death when trapped inside refrigerators inadvertently closed on them. Kittens are particularly curious and may easily climb inside, searching for the source of that wonderful odor their sensitive nose has detected. Dishwashers may be equally tempting, especially if they are filled with dirty dishes.

Sharp objects such as knives should be put away and never left out when you are not in the kitchen. After washing the kitchen floor, wait until it is dry before allowing your cat to walk on it. The chemicals, many of them poisonous, can stick to a cat's paws, to be licked off at bath time. This can make a cat quite sick . . . or worse.

## Plants

Despite the fact that they are carnivores, cats enjoy a bit of salad now and then. In the wild cats chew on grass to help aid in their digestion, but in the house the only greens that are usually available are your houseplants. Providing your cat with his own indoor garden consisting of kitty greens and catnip (preplanted pots can often be purchased from pet supply stores) will help your cat avoid your more treasured greenery. But even with these ready-made kitty salad bowls, many cats still prefer to munch on your favorite fern or use

### Common Toxic Plants

| | | |
|---|---|---|
| Arrowhead vine | Daffodil | Marijuana |
| Boston ivy | Dieffenbachia | Mistletoe |
| Caladium | English ivy | Nutmeg |
| Christmas berries | Holly | Philodendron |
| Chrysanthemum | Ivy | Poppy |
| Creeping Charlie | Jasmine | Spider mum |
| Creeping fig | Laurel | |

### Online Resources

For more on various poisonous plants:

www.ansci.cornell.edu/plants

www.cfsan.fda.gov/~djw/plantox.html

www.aggie-horticulture.tamu.edu/plantanswers/publications/poison/poison.html

the soil as a litter box, which is bad for the cat as well as the plant. For this reason, plants should be removed or kept well out of reach, particularly poisonous plants. You may also wish to spray a bitter, nontoxic substance on the plants as a deterrent. Pet supply stores and your veterinarian can recommend sprays made especially for use on plants.

Enclosing the plants behind glass or screens can also help to keep your cat from them. It's a good idea, however, to find out in advance if your plants are toxic to cats. The table on page 27 lists some common household plants that are toxic. There are many others, so check to be sure.

## Chemicals

Keep all chemicals out of your cat's reach at all times. It's important to know that antifreeze is particularly dangerous because it contains the toxic chemical ethylene glycol and has a sweet taste cats are drawn to. That's why antifreeze is best kept where it belongs—outside, in proper containers—and spilled antifreeze should be cleaned up immediately (as with all chemicals) and the cleaning rags disposed of properly, in bins with tight-fitting lids. Propylene glycol–based antifreeze is a bit more expensive, but it's less toxic to pets.

Aerosol sprays should never be used around the cat or around the cat's eating area. If you have your carpets cleaned, keep your cat off them until they are safely dry.

If your house requires fumigation, the cats would be best kept at a friend's or in a boarding facility for the day until it is safe for them to return. After fumigating, all eating surfaces and dishes should be cleaned and washed with nontoxic detergent, the litter boxes should be cleaned, and any areas the cats frequent should be cleaned as well.

## The Bathroom

The bathroom is another room in your house that is filled with dangers, particularly for a kitten. Deodorants, perfumes, tub and toilet cleaners, and curling irons should be kept out of your cat's reach at all times.

Human medicines should always be kept away from cats. A cat's metabolism is much different from ours, and medicines that may help us can kill a cat. For example, aspirin can be fatal to cats. Ibuprofen is also deadly. So keep all human pain relievers away from cats.

Cats love to drink from toilets, maybe because the fresh, cold water is always being renewed. Some cats will come running at the sound of the toilet flushing, anxious for a cool drink. But caution is advised. Toilet bowl cleaner inserts, if used, should be kept out of your cat's reach—as should the affected water in the bowl. Most toilet bowl inserts are toxic to cats, although 2000 Flushes brand now has an insert that will not harm pets should they drink from the bowl (look on the back of the package for details). Although this may be the case, however, it is still best to keep the lid down.

Small kittens have been known to fall into toilet bowls and drown, so even if you do not use toilet bowl chemicals, the lid should be kept down. Your best bet is to be sure kitty always has fresh, clean, cold water available at all times in his own bowl, rather than the toilet bowl. Affordable cat water fountains are available at pet supply stores in several varieties; they provide cats with fresh, filtered drinking water at all times. If a reservoir for extra water is available separately, I recommend it. Other than changing the filter and cleaning the fountain every so often, there is little more maintenance than making sure the unit remains full of water.

## Windows and Balconies

Some cats take delight not only in sitting in windows, but in trying to get out of them. Windows throughout your house should have

## Holidays

During the holidays, extra precautions must be taken to ensure your cat's safety. Any breakable, toxic, or harmful ornaments, plants, or knickknacks should be kept out of the cat's reach or not used at all. Strings of popcorn or beads, as well as the string and needles to make these garlands, can be a threat to your cat's safety.

A rambunctious kitten or cat should be kept away from any decorations or Christmas tree when you're not at home to supervise. And be extra careful with electrical cords and lights.

*Take extra precautions around the holidays.*

secure screens with a strong mesh so your cat cannot tear them or push them out.

City dwellers, beware! Because of a cat's natural grace and tendency to land on his feet, many people who live in apartment buildings think their cats will not jump or will know to stay away from heights. But hundreds of cats every year are killed or injured by falls out of windows. This phenomenon is so common that it even has a name: high-rise syndrome. Not only do you want to be sure your cat can't get outside, but you want to secure the screens so they cannot be pushed out. Never leave a window open without a screen.

Balconies should also be cat-proofed. Wire mesh covering on the balcony rails can prevent a cat from slipping off or jumping through the rails.

## Other Areas

A cat's legs and body are built for leaping, running, and jumping, and cats enjoy viewing their territory from atop high places. Thus, an energetic kitten or cat may spell trouble for anything glass, ceramic, or crystal in your house. In an attempt to pounce on that unsuspecting bug or imaginary mouse, a kitten or cat may run and jump onto tabletops, knocking down anything in his path. My cats sometimes even manage to get on top of the curio cabinet in the living room via the top of the television.

Your home is your cat's playhouse and, as the owner of an indoor cat, you must safeguard your valuables. Even if you train your cat not to jump up onto certain areas, there will still be a time, particularly with a new pet who has not yet learned the rules, that your cat will find these areas irresistible. Keep breakables in closed curio cabinets and hutches and, as I have learned the hard way, don't place anything valuable on top of them.

Fireplaces and kerosene heaters should be covered with safety screens. It is in your cat's best interest to err on the side of caution and make sure the cat cannot come into contact with or be exposed to hot embers or sparks. Wood-burning stoves usually pose little danger to cats, but some cats will sleep so close to a wood-burning stove that their fur becomes hot to the touch.

The paint in older homes can be dangerous, since the lead in old paint can poison a cat who eats it. If the paint is chipping and you have the means, repaint before your new cat comes home.

Electrical cords hanging within reach or running along the floor are just too tempting. Some cats love to chew and explore what to them is an interesting object. If you have a cat who likes to chew, keep your electrical cords bound tightly and wrapped in aluminum foil or some other material that is unattractive to cats. Cords can also be run above doors, secured to the wall along baseboards or in some other way fastened out of your pet's reach. (Do not, however, place cords beneath furniture or carpets, or stick tacks or staples into the cord, because this can be dangerous for you.) Pet supply stores and veterinarians also sell sprays with a bitter taste that can be sprayed on electrical cords, but make sure these are safe to use on the wires before you buy them.

Just as electrical cords can be dangerous, so can outlets. In countries such as the United States where most outlets do not have on-off safety switches, electrical outlets that are not in use should be kept covered if your cat is particularly curious. Childproof outlet covers are available at most hardware and department stores.

The clothes dryer can be another hazard for a cat. It's warm and cozy, and many cats will curl up unseen inside. Always check your clothes dryer before putting clothes in and turning it on, and before shutting the door.

## Bringing Kitty Home

At first, your cat may be apprehensive about being in a new place. This is normal. If your new pet is a kitten, then most likely he has not been away from Momma long. If your cat's an adult, he's likely to be more wary of change than a kitten. Depending on the cat's personality and past, he may run and hide, crouch low to the ground and explore, or take immediate charge of the household. In any case, leave the cat alone for awhile in the beginning to let him grow accustomed to your home at his own pace.

I'll look first at how to introduce your cat to a household with no other pets. Later in this chapter I'll discuss what you can do to welcome your cat into a multicat household.

## Shy Cats

Maybe you acquired your cat as a stray, or maybe the cat is feral or came from an abusive situation before you adopted him. If this is the case, your new cat may be more shy and apprehensive about this new place he has been brought into. Although almost all cats may be shy in the first few days, a cat from one of these situations may take longer to adjust and will need more love and reassurance than an outgoing cat.

More than likely, a shy cat will hide when you first bring him home. Leave the cat alone for awhile and go about your business. Don't have any parties or large gatherings of people in your home for awhile, as this may frighten the cat more. He will need time to learn that you are trustworthy.

Your new cat will likely choose a hiding place where he feels safe—maybe inside a closet, under a desk, or behind a bed. If the cat won't come out of the haven he has chosen after a day has passed, place his food, water, and litter box near the spot he has chosen (make sure this place is safe and comfortable; if not, move the cat to a more convenient location). This will give the cat more reassurance that he doesn't have to expose himself in the open to take care of his needs. When you can, sit with the cat, pet him, and speak in a soothing tone (but do not allow a crowd to gather around, and never allow children to run around near the cat).

Don't give up hope. When your cat is ready, he will come out and explore. This may take anywhere from a day or two to weeks, maybe months, depending on the cat. When I first brought home my cat Precious, she was so shy that she stayed hidden whenever anyone was in the house. She would only come out to eat or use the litter box at night or when no one was home. It took six months before she was trusting enough to mingle with the rest of the family. After that, she would only hide when company came. Now, years and lots of love later, she trusts and loves everyone in the house and even visits with most strangers.

Eventually, your cat's natural curiosity and instincts will bring him out of his shell. Not all cats will learn to trust strangers, but with the proper introductions, time, and patience, they will love you.

## Apprehensive Cats

Some cats will be curious yet apprehensive about entering a new home. These cats will generally crouch low to the ground as they explore their new environment, seeming to contradict their own movements. As with very shy cats, leave the cat alone at first and don't have any company or parties until the cat is comfortable. You don't want to frighten an apprehensive cat into becoming a shy cat.

After a few hours, show your new pet where his food, water, and litter box will be kept. You may have to show these items to the cat several times in the next few days, particularly with a new kitten, but cats are quick learners. It will be easier if you have other cats in the house, as they will lead the newcomer to where these essentials are located.

## Outgoing Cats

Some cats will need practically no introduction to your home. They are the outgoing types who will come in and take over almost immediately. These cats seem to learn more quickly where their litter box is, and particularly where that delicious food is kept. It is not that they are more intelligent than a shy or apprehensive cat; they are simply more extroverted and have no qualms about going for what they want.

However, even if your new cat seems immediately at home in his new surroundings, he will still need guidance and adjustment time for those first few days. It is still wise not to allow parties or excessive noise, and always show a new cat or kitten where his litter box, food, and water will be kept.

# Introducing People

Think from your cat's point of view. You are small and just taken away from a familiar place, only to arrive in a completely new location filled with unfamiliar scents, sights, and sounds. The last thing you would want is a large party and groups of people staring at you as if they are expecting you to perform for them.

*After* your cat has become accustomed to, and accepted, his new home, it will be time to introduce other family members, pets, and house rules. But remember, always allow your new pet time to adjust. This period of adjustment will vary with each cat. As I mentioned before, shy and apprehensive cats should be left alone, except for love and reassurance from you, until they're ready to wander out on their own. When you feel your cat is ready, introduce people and other pets—slowly, if possible.

## Family Members, Including Children

The procedure for introductions will depend on the individual cat's personality. For shy cats it is best to introduce adults first, one at a time. If the adult has already been spending time with the cat while he is in hiding, then introductions may not be necessary. If not, or if the person is a stranger to your home, the adult should always sit on the floor before an introduction is made. This position is less threatening to the cat and brings the person to the cat's level. The adult should stroke the cat gently and speak soothingly until the cat is comfortable. With some cats this may take several tries. Never force the cat to stay if he does not want to. This will only frighten a shy animal more. Also, make no sudden moves or loud noises around the cat.

This type of introduction also works with apprehensive and outgoing cats but should not take as long to accomplish, as long as nothing frightens the animal. Always be gentle with any introductions, no matter what the cat's personality.

I recommend that you do not acquire an extremely shy cat if you have young children, because kids are naturally rambunctious and cannot understand how important it is to be calm and quiet around such a cat. Children will be excited about the new addition to the family and will want to play. This seemingly harmless activity may have serious consequences for a shy and withdrawn cat.

However, if a cat of this type has fallen into your care and you have young children, it is very important to supervise all activity in the cat's presence. Hold the child's hand while you both stroke the cat gently, showing the proper way to pet a cat. Explain that this is a living being with feelings and not a toy. Never let several children gang up at once on any cat, particularly a shy cat. Teach them to pet the cat one at a time and quietly.

Even with outgoing cats, a child should be taught to be gentle and how to handle and stroke the cat. Even a harmless ear or tail tug can result in painful scratches to the child. The difference with an outgoing cat, however, is that he will likely grow accustomed to the noises and activity level of children more easily and quickly than a shy or even an apprehensive cat.

## Picking Up a Cat

Teach all children the proper way to pick up a cat: by placing one hand under the cat's hind end and the other hand just under and behind the front paws, then lifting gently. This should be done with the child sitting down at first, so the child does not drop the cat and can get used to the procedure. And make sure children understand they should not pick up the cat unless it is absolutely necessary, and they certainly should not carry the cat around the house.

A cat should never be acquired solely for the purpose of teaching a child responsibility. If your child forgets to do the dishes, they can pile up for a day or two in the sink. But a neglected cat suffers needlessly. Always supervise to be sure the cat is fed properly, fresh water is given, and the litter box is scooped or changed regularly. Remember, young kittens may scratch or bite when they play. A child should learn how to tell when a kitten (or a cat) has had enough and wants to be left alone.

## Cats and Babies

I'm still amazed at the number of people who think they must give up their cat because they are expecting a baby. This is partly due to a few myths that still persist about cats and babies. Pregnant women are often told they must give up their cats because of the threat of toxoplasmosis, a disease that can cause birth defects. It's true that toxoplasmosis can be spread to pregnant women through the feces of a cat, but outdoor cats are much more of a threat, and in any case the problem can easily be avoided. If you are pregnant, either avoid cleaning the litter box or wear rubber gloves when doing so, and always wash your hands thoroughly afterward. It's that simple.

Jealousy (on the part of the cat) is another commonly cited problem that is easily avoided. Your cat is part of the family, and some cats may become jealous when a new baby comes into the home (see chapter 3 for more on jealousy). If possible, you should introduce your cat to baby sights, sounds, and smells before the baby actually arrives. You can set up a tape recording with the sound of a baby crying, play with your cat around baby toys, and maybe create a "mock day with the baby" where you do the kinds of things you'll do after the baby arrives. Open up packages of baby products, such as wipes, lotions, and shampoos, and dab them on yourself before the baby is born so these smells become familiar.

Once the baby comes home, don't forget to give your cat plenty of attention. It's probably a good idea to keep the cat out of the baby's room and away from the crib unless you are there to supervise. Cats love to curl up where it's warm, and this could be in the crib with the baby. As much as your cat may be trying to show affection to the new child (cats can and do fall in love with babies), a ten-pound cat lying atop a small infant can smother a child.

The fact that cats love to knead with their paws to show contentment, lie on top of a child's warm body, and at times taste the milk that may be left behind on a child's mouth, has been the genesis of many strange myths (such as the myth that a cat will "suck a baby's breath away," which is completely false). Once the child is old enough and big enough to handle the cat's weight and to knock the cat off if he or she chooses, then the main caution is to prevent scratches or bites by teaching the child how to behave around a cat.

## Meeting Other Cats

Introducing your new kitten or cat to other household pets is a different matter. You cannot explain to your other pets how to behave around the new family member, so introductions must be made carefully. All cats react differently to new arrivals. Some will be accepting, others indifferent, and still others defensive.

My neutered male cat Pounce hisses with the arrival of new adult cats, but loves kittens. I once fostered many kittens before they were placed in homes, and Pounce would take it upon himself to make them feel right at home while they were here, even allowing them to suckle his belly fur while he bathed them—just like a mother cat. Most males are not as maternal as Pounce, but some females may be. I've even known people whose kittens "nurse" on the dog.

If you are getting a new kitten or cat as a companion for a resident kitten or cat, try to find one with the same personality, manner, and activity level, and near the same age. Many experts suggest getting a male cat for a female and vice versa. However, once cats are altered (castrated or spayed) it usually does not matter. Many shelters nowadays alter kittens through an early spay/neuter program, so you will not have to worry about having it done later. Spaying or neutering a young kitten is not dangerous to the animal and is becoming more common as a way to reduce the numbers of unwanted kittens.

It is easier to introduce kittens into a household with other cats than it is to introduce an adult cat. Even so, whether you adopt a kitten or a cat, the following method is suggested. This introduction method can take anywhere from a couple of hours to a day, depending on the reaction of the cats to one another.

Place the newcomer in a separate room with food, water, and a litter box. If the new cat is in a carrier (which he should be) and is reluctant to come out, allow him to stay there. Leave the door to the carrier open and leave the room.

Cats use scent as a communication tool, "reading" the pheromones secreted from another cat's glands. Letting your resident cat(s) sniff around the door of the room the new cat is in will help the cats identify one another before meeting face to face. Do not be surprised if, despite the door between them, there is much hissing and spitting among all cats. This is normal and should not cause you much alarm. If a towel or a blanket came with the newcomer (or anything else with the new cat's scent on it), set it down for your other cat(s) to inspect.

Feeding resident cats near the base of the door will help them associate something pleasant with the new cat's scent. Give your resident cats plenty of attention during this time so they will not feel abandoned. Visit the new cat frequently as well for calm reassurance.

When all the cats have relaxed, move your new cat to a different location in the house. Allow resident cats to enter the room your new cat was in, so they may sniff around and become more accustomed to the scent. If you have the space in your house and the time to spend, you may want to try moving your new cat to a different room each day for several days until his scent fills the house before allowing him to mingle face to face with your other cat(s).

Once the cats begin to appear more comfortable with one another's scent, try placing your new cat in a carrier with a barred door and let him and your other cat(s) smell each other through the door. Again, expect plenty of hissing and growling.

The next step is to let your new cat or kitten mingle with resident cats, but keep a close eye on them. Feeding them together might help. Some experts recommend placing a dot of butter on the new cat to help persuade resident cats to lick him and learn to accept the new cat. However, never force newly acquainted cats together.

If you acquire a kitten and have an adult cat, watch them closely. A spunky kitten may pester an older cat relentlessly. When I first brought my cat Pounce into the house as an eight-week-old kitten, he would romp around attacking the adult cats even as they were trying to sleep. Some of the cats were very patient with him, others were not. Even as an adult cat, Pounce is rambunctious (some cats don't outgrow kittenhood as quickly as others) and he still tries to play with the older cats, whether they want to or not. Now they are accustomed to his ways, and he usually receives one of two typical responses from them. Either he'll be humored with play, or he'll find a paw swiping across his face followed by a hind-end view of the offended cat walking away.

An indoor cat who has been an only cat may be even less patient with the antics of a young kitten than cats in a multicat family are. Keeping the kitten busy with toys and games, or acquiring two kittens, might help take the pressure off the older cat. However, in some cases a kitten will actually bring out the frisky in an older cat. Some of my older, more sedentary cats acted like kittens again after Pounce came into the house.

And then there are those rare instances, unfortunately, when the resident cat(s) will simply not accept a newcomer. This is more likely to happen with an only cat who has been alone for quite some time. My brother recently adopted a beautiful shorthaired tortoiseshell cat named Zoie from the shelter where I volunteer. Even though she had spent a few years of her life at the shelter with many other cats, Zoie never really got along with any of them, except one—a shorthaired orange and white male. Since my brother works two jobs and lives alone, he was afraid Zoie might be lonely while he was away, so he decided, after he had her for a week, that he would adopt the male Zoie had gotten along with to keep her company. Apparently Zoie, who had taken over my brother's home from the moment she arrived, did not agree with this idea. The cat she got along with so well at the shelter was suddenly an intruder in "her" home. She hid constantly, hissed whenever the male (whom my brother named Shemp) tried to play with her, and her loving nature turned aggressive.

It was unfair to Shemp for my brother to keep him, as it was obvious after a week that this situation was not going to work. Shemp, being a social, playful cat, could not understand why Zoie wanted nothing to do with him and, with my brother gone most of the time, he grew lonely. It was a painful decision, but my brother gave Shemp back to the shelter (where he was later adopted to a wonderful family and receives the love and play he requires), and Zoie took over the house once more. Her loving nature returned and she is again happy.

Some cats simply prefer to be alone. Although Zoie plays with my brother as if he were another cat ("attacking" his arms and pouncing on him), she still prefers being head cat in the household. My brother is all she needs, and she is perfectly happy this way. And my brother, who really only wanted one cat anyway, found the perfect roommate.

Give your new cat time to adjust (ideally two to four weeks) and see how things go. If plenty of time has passed and it becomes obvious that one or more of your cats will simply never get along, that the cats are completely miserable in one another's company, you may need to return the new cat (if possible). As painful as this decision is, it's better than allowing the cats to live in misery together.

If returning the cat is not an option and you are determined to find a way to get these two cats to at least tolerate each other, you may wish to try a cat behaviorist. Yes, there are therapists for animals and sometimes they can work with you and the cats to come up with a solution. Ask your veterinarian or a shelter professional if they know of any cat behaviorists in your area.

## Introducing Other Animals

Introducing new cats to other animals, particularly dogs, requires more caution than when introducing a cat to another cat. When you bring a new cat into a home that already has other animals, your priority should be the safety and security of all involved. You don't want your dog to injure your cat, but you also don't want the cat injuring your hamster or bird—or dog.

### Dogs

Some cats and dogs seem to be natural friends, others natural enemies. Pounce, odd one that he is, absolutely loves my Doberman Pinscher, Wolfe, and my mother's Labrador Retriever, Bridget. Pounce has been seen kneading the dogs, curling up beside them, and washing their faces daily. But not all cats will take to dogs as Pounce does. If you are introducing your new cat to a dog who has never been around cats before, introductions will require care and patience.

Introduce the cat at the dog's eye level, holding both carefully. If the dog seems agitated or aggressive, remove the cat and try again another time. Never leave the cat and dog unsupervised until they are

*Dogs and cats can get along just fine.*

*Rats are fun to watch. Be sure they are in a tightly closed cage, though.*

perfectly comfortable and accustomed to one another. Even an overly playful larger dog who is accustomed to cats may inadvertently injure a cat or kitten, so close supervision is essential.

There are occasionally times when the dog and cat will not become accustomed to each other, no matter how much time and patience you have. If this is the case, it would be in the cat's best interest to find him a more suitable home.

Usually cats who have grown up with a dog or a puppy are more likely to become friends with another dog. If you acquire a puppy, things should go a bit smoother with introductions. A puppy, like a kitten, has not yet fully developed the instincts he will have as an adult, and the most trouble you will probably run into is the puppy's unending energy. A puppy will see your cat as another puppy to play with. Although a cat is intelligent enough and able to defend himself if the puppy becomes too rowdy, a declawed cat, an ill cat, or a more-sedentary cat may not be able to defend himself or get away from the puppy's advances. Be careful that the puppy (particularly a large breed) does not harm the cat in his enthusiasm to play, or wear an older cat out with constant demands.

## Birds, Reptiles, and Rodents

It is not necessary to actually introduce your new cat to these types of pets unless they will be interacting regularly. Even so, these pets should be kept in secure cages and out of your cat's reach.

As with dogs, use extreme caution when introducing these types of pets to your cat. A cat's natural instincts are to play with or even kill these animals, depending on the cat's background and personality. Many cats who are raised indoors seem to lose some of the hunt-and-kill drive, but they still retain the instinct to chase and even catch prey. I have pet rats and I allow them to interact with some of my cats. Precious, when she was younger, retained a strong hunting drive, but now that she is older and has been living indoors for seventeen years, her main focus is on getting as much attention as she can.

Some cats will never be able to interact with "prey" animals safely. Others will mother these pets and treat them as if they were the cat's own babies. To introduce a rodent, bird, or reptile to your new cat, hold the pet carefully and watch the cat's response. If his instinct seems to be to attack, take the animal away. Otherwise, let them interact and keep a close watch.

*Never* leave a cat unsupervised with a small animal, no matter how good the relationship between them. Be sure your pet is secure in a cage that nothing can get out of or into.

## Ferrets

I put ferrets in their own section because ferrets and cats, unlike rodents and cats, are not natural enemies. Ferrets and cats usually get along great with little introduction. In my experience, however, it's usually the ferret, with his playful and rambunctious nature, who intimidates the cat. Make sure the cat is not frightened of the ferret and the ferret is comfortable around the cat.

*Even fish can be great companions to a cat, as long as the fish tank lid is cat-proof.*

Ferrets have extremely tough skin and can play very rough, not understanding that the cat's skin isn't as rugged as their own. Generally, more active cats will get along best with ferrets. My cats Pounce and Shadow are so rambunctious that the ferrets have the same energy level. When I take the ferrets out, those cats are right there wanting to play with them. At times Pounce gets too rough even for the ferrets.

As with any other animal, supervise play activities carefully until the animals are accustomed to one another and you are positive no harm will come to either pet.

## Carrier Training

More than likely, your new cat will be coming home in a carrier. Depending on where you acquire your cat, the carrier may come with the animal or you may need to buy one in advance. There are many kinds of carriers on the market, but airline-approved plastic carriers with wire doors have proven to be among the best types of carriers available.

The chances are good your cat will not like being confined in a carrier unless he was trained to accept one. Kittens are easiest to acclimate to carriers simply because kittens are impressionable and the attitudes they learn early on generally remain with them for life. Cats can learn to accept a ride in a carrier as long as they have not already learned to fear and hate carriers.

Generally, the only association cats have with their carriers is a trip to the vet—fear and shots. Negative associations. The object behind teaching a cat not to fear the carrier as much as he fears going to the vet is to teach him a positive association before he must be carted off to the veterinarian. To do this, you must introduce your cat or kitten to a carrier slowly and accompany it with positive reinforcement.

Although cats don't like to be confined, they do like to sleep in small, confining spaces. If given the opportunity, some cats will even sleep in their carriers. Try simply leaving the carrier open, with a soft towel inside, in a location where the cat is likely to want to curl up and sleep. You can also try playing with your cat in or near his carrier. Place catnip toys inside and even food treats.

Once your cat seems calm around the carrier, try closing the door and then opening it again. Do this regularly, every day, closing the door for longer and longer periods until the cat can remain calmly in the carrier for ten minutes or so. Next, lift the carrier with the cat in it, and carry it around the house a bit. Once your cat is comfortable with this process, try taking the carrier, cat inside and door firmly locked, outside for a small walk around the yard. All the while, speak to the cat and reassure him that this is fun and that no harm will come to him.

Don't expect your cat to accept his carrier in one day. This should be an ongoing process, and it could take weeks, perhaps months, depending on the cat, for him to willingly go into a carrier. Eventually, you can move the process up a step to taking the cat into

*Cats can learn to love their carriers.*

the car. Set the carrier on the front seat and start the engine. Have toys and treats ready to distract your cat if he seems nervous. Don't open the carrier; offer the treats through the bars in the door, or wave a feather toy in front of the door for the cat to watch and bat at.

Next, take a little trip with the cat. Just a short trip at first, five or ten minutes. Make the trips longer and longer; maybe one trip per week. Don't overdo it.

Even though your cat now accepts the carrier and maybe even goes into it willingly, don't limit your trips just to the vet, or the cat will eventually figure out that is what the carrier is for and will learn to fear it. Since most cats will only need about one trip to the vet a year, that gives you plenty of time to take your cat for the occasional fun trip. Don't forget the treats and toys, even on trips to the vet.

## Setting House Rules

It has been widely stated that cats are incapable of learning house rules. This belief is fueled by cats' tendency to want things done their way. It is also not wholly true. Cats are intelligent animals and are quite capable of learning rules and even tricks, when taught properly and with patience.

Persistence, patience, and consistency are the keys to teaching house rules to cats. It is important to remember that any rule (such as not jumping on counters) you want your kitten to follow in adulthood must be taught right from the start. Try not to give in on the rules just because the kitten is cute or the cat is new to the house, only to punish the cat later when the novelty of owning him has worn off. A cat does not understand why he was allowed on the table or counter as a kitten and is punished for the same behavior as a cat. You'll want your cat to know the rules you've established right away.

When I turn the lights out at night, I generally am sharing my bed with at least two or three cats in various locations around me. I love it, but not everyone wants their cat to share their bed. Maybe you have mild allergies and need to keep the cat away from your sleeping area, or maybe you have a particularly rambunctious cat who loves to chase toes in the middle of the night. Whatever the reason, simply keeping the door closed does not always work, unless the cat has been well trained from kittenhood to stay out and not try to bang the door down when it is closed.

Cats hate closed doors. Their natural curiosity makes them want to get on the other side, even if they know what is there. But, as with any other rule, teaching the cat to stay out is a task that requires patience and persistence. A cat who has always been allowed in the bedroom and suddenly isn't anymore will probably not accept this change lightly. He wants to be with you and does not understand why he suddenly can't. He may wail and cry outside the door, scratch and try to stick his paws under the door, as if he can lift the door up enough to slip under. You can try keeping the cat in another room, but chances are his wailing will keep you up anyway. This is a good example of why you must decide what rules to set forth for your cat before you bring him home.

## Play and Messages

Often what is viewed as aggression, whether among cats or between a cat and a person, is really cat play or the cat's way of relating a message the only way he knows how. Some cats, if they do not wish to be petted at that moment, will suddenly attack your hand for what seems like no apparent reason. In play, sometimes a cat will run at you from out of nowhere and "ambush" your leg. If you do not like this behavior, you must work with the cat at as young an age as possible to stop it. A quick squirt of water in the cat's direction (not right in the face), if you know when the cat will "attack," can give puss the message that this is inappropriate behavior. Often, stomping your feet or yelling at your cat will halt the behavior quickly, but with some cats this may cause a neurotic behavior or fear of your feet–or you.

## Corrections

When training or correcting a cat, never hit or use extreme physical force. A cat will not associate the punishment with the crime, and may grow fearful of you while retaining the behavior you wished to stop. A good correction tool is a water pistol or spray bottle filled with water (please, do not squirt your cat right in the face). Most cats hate being sprayed with water and will quickly learn that getting up on the counter or scratching your sofa will result in a squirt.

But the water trick only works when you catch your cat in the act. Do not correct a cat or kitten for a mistake he made a minute or an hour before. Even if you drag your cat to the scene of the crime, he will have no idea what the correction is for–cats simply don't associate events past and present the way we do.

If, however, your cat learns to stay off the counters only when you are around, you might want to keep him in another room when you are away, at least until he learns the appropriate rules. You can also try placing a substance on the inappropriate area that is unpleasant for the cat to walk on, such as aluminum foil or double-sided tape.

## Cat Beds

If you want your cat to have his own bed, there are many to choose from. Most pet supply stores sell cat beds, and there is usually a vendor at every cat show who sells them as well. Cat beds range from pads you can place anywhere you wish to wicker baskets or elaborately decorated and colored cat "palaces." Whichever bed you choose, it should be soft, comfortable, and washable.

Some beds have cedar mattresses to repel fleas. However, they are not recommended, as cedar can cause respiratory problems in some cats.

Keep your cat's bed clean and dry; cats are meticulously clean, and most are opposed to sleeping in soiled areas. This includes cleaning the frame of the bed as well as the pad. You can buy a bed with removable pads that can be thrown in the washing machine, or you can place a towel inside the bed. Some beds are entirely washable.

A clean cardboard box with a towel or small blanket inside also makes a pretty good cat bed. It's not as decorative as a bed you'd buy, but your cat won't mind.

You cannot make your cat sleep in a particular location, so placing the cat bed where the cat spends most of his sleep time will help ensure the bed is used. Sprinkling catnip on the bed and playing with the cat in it will also help create a pleasant association with the bed. You can also make or buy a pad with a zipper on one end that opens so you can place catnip inside it. These can be placed inside a regular cat bed to help attract your cat to it.

## Crate Training

Crate training is usually associated with dogs, but kittens can be crate-trained as well. A crate is a cage, either an all-wire cage or a large airline-approved carrier (usually a combination of wire and plastic). An adult cat who has not been in a cage before will most likely not accept a crate and does not need one, so it is best to limit crate training to kittens. The crate should be large enough so the kitten has room to play, and it should also accommodate a small litter box, food and water dishes, and the kitten's bed. The largest-size dog crate works best.

Why would you want to crate-train your kitten? For times when you are not at home or if you want a good night's sleep, crate training is a good idea. Kittens want to play at all hours and get into mischief frequently. Crate training will give you peace of mind and prevent the kitten from harming himself when you are not there to supervise. Crate training also teaches a kitten to eventually accept a cat carrier.

Kittens do not resent being confined and will generally sleep in their crate even when the door is left open. The crate should be lined with a soft towel or blanket, which should be kept clean and dry. Place the crate in a draft-free area away from crowds and traffic in your home.

Acclimate the kitten to his crate by keeping the door open on the first day and showing the kitten where the crate is and that it contains food and water. Place the kitten inside and play with him, speaking softly. Try closing the door, but if the kitten seems to panic, open it again. You do not want any negative associations with the crate, which will eventually become your cat's own special place. You can continue trying the next day.

If the kitten seems reasonably content, walk away for a few minutes, then return a few moments later and open the door. Continue this throughout the day, leaving the kitten for longer and longer periods of time. At night, place kitty in the crate after playtime and when he is tired. Walk away, leaving him alone with his thoughts. Make no fuss, even if he cries, and soon your precious little bundle of fur will be sound asleep. Make sure your kitten has plenty of playtime and family interaction outside the crate most of the time.

Never use the crate for punishment or keep the kitten in it for extended periods of time, such as when you go away. Also, if you work full time, your kitten should not be kept in the crate all night and all day. Find another way to keep the kitten out of trouble, such as confining him to a large room equipped with toys, food, water, and litter box, and with all dangers removed.

As your kitten grows, learns the rules, and becomes less rambunctious, allow him more and more time out of the crate until you no longer need it. A full-grown cat usually will not get into the trouble a kitten will, and should not be confined. Once your cat no longer uses the crate, you can remove it or leave it open all the time (your cat may prefer to sleep there). I have crate-trained three of my adult cats from kittenhood, and all still sleep in any crate or carrier they can get themselves into.

# Acclimating Your Cat to the Indoors

Each cat is unique, as are their circumstances before they came to you. Many times, this previous situation plays a vital role in shaping the cat's personality and will have an effect on how well the cat adapts to indoor life.

Once your cat has become accustomed to your home and settled in as one of the family, you will want to take into account the cat's previous situation, if known, when you decide how best to acclimate him to life as a house cat. Following are some of the most basic situations a cat may have faced, and the best methods of getting your cat accustomed to being indoors all the time. Whether you've acquired a kitten who has never seen the outdoors or an adult cat who has lived outside all his life, with love and patience you can teach your cat to live happily in the safety of home.

## Kitten—Never Been Outdoors

This is the simplest situation to deal with. A kitten adjusts much more readily to new situations than an adult cat, and one who has never been outdoors will not be constantly trying to escape. In this situation, you simply acclimate the new kitten to your home, as described earlier in this chapter.

There are some kittens, however, especially as they reach adolescence and become more curious, who will try to get out when they see you going in and out of the door. Their curious nature will make them want to know what is so fascinating that keeps you wandering out there. I had this problem with my cat Taffy for many years, until she got out and discovered life was a lot better indoors. Sometimes a cat outgrows this curiosity, but why wait and risk an escape when you can do something about it now?

One way to deal with this problem, besides giving the cat plenty of toys to keep him occupied and cat trees to climb on, is to make a rule that outside doors are an inappropriate area for the cat. A water squirt bottle is effective here. Stand outside the door and open the door a small crack. When your curious feline comes too close, spray the cat with water, then slam the door. This, combined with a verbal reprimand or even slamming the door hard whenever the cat gets near, should help keep him away. Let your cat know this is one of the rules: Doors are off-limits. But remember, as with any training, be patient and consistent, and never hit your cat with anything.

You can also try the treat or toy method, combined with positive reinforcement. When you are getting ready to leave the house, have a few treats or a toy ready. If your cat looks as though he is eyeing the door, toss the treat or toy in another direction, as far away from the door as possible. Leave while the cat is distracted with his treats. Be careful you do not do this too close to the door, because some cats might start to associate the door with the treats. You want your cat to associate staying away from the door with getting a reward.

Many kittens will decide to make a mad dash for the door when they see it open. This is a behavior that will have to be prevented. The best thing is to be one step ahead of the kitten. If you know he is going to do this, either use a squirt bottle of water or close the door quickly (*before* he gets to it; be careful he does *not* get closed in the door!). You can train your kitten not to do this from the start by setting him up, knowing what he is going to do before he does it, and squirting him with water as he nears the door. You can also try a bit of trickery. Have a carrier ready on the other side of the door. Unless he is extremely fast or you know he will see it in time and leap over it, you can place it so that as he dashes out the door, he ends up inside the carrier. A few of these episodes and he might rethink where that door leads.

## Kitten—Previously Lived Outdoors

Although kittens adjust quite easily to most situations, one who has spent a great deal of time or all of his life outdoors (such as a barn, feral, or stray cat) may need a period of adjustment to accept his sudden confinement indoors. Even at a young age, cats become accustomed to their environment. Acclimating a strictly outdoor kitten to indoor life will require patience and persistence.

First, you want to go through all the steps outlined in the previous section ("Kitten—Never Been Outdoors") to acclimate the kitten to your house and to teach him that the door to the outside is an inappropriate location.

As an adolescent, a young outdoor cat might be more persistent at trying to escape than a young kitten. They know what goes on outdoors and are usually not afraid of what's out there. Keeping a close eye on all those who come in and out of your house will be crucial in the beginning. Your new kitten or adolescent cat might try the dart-quickly-out-the-door-when-it-opens routine. Let everyone who comes in or out know about your cat, so they can be *very* careful around the door. Combine this with plenty of indoor activities such as toys, cat trees to climb, window perches, balls to chase, and so on. Once the kitten has grown into adulthood, he will be plenty satisfied with indoor life and will most likely forget about trying to escape.

Sometimes adopting two kittens around the same age will keep their minds off wanting to go out, as they will be too busy playing with each other.

## Adult Cat—Never Been Outdoors

This is the easiest situation for acclimating your new pet. An adult cat who has never been outdoors knows he's not missing anything.

The cat will already be accustomed to life indoors and will need very little adjustment. All you have to do in a situation like this is to acclimate your new pet to your house, make sure he knows where the food, water, and litter box are, and teach him the house rules.

## Adult Cat—Previously Allowed Outdoors

Sylvia was a stray outdoor cat who lived in the woods behind a yacht club. One day she just strolled down the dock, tail held high, as if she owned the place. We already had eleven cats in our house when Sylvia "found" my mother and stepfather. They took her onto their boat, which was docked at the yacht club the week they were there on summer vacation.

Probably because she had always been an outdoor cat, Sylvia had no idea what to do with the litter box my stepfather placed in the boat for her. Instead, she woke him in the middle of the night so he could take her outside to do her business. When the week was up, and after she had been checked over by the veterinarian who had a practice beside the yacht club, my mother and stepfather brought Sylvia home.

In the beginning we were concerned that she might not accept her sudden confinement indoors. We underestimated her. Sylvia took to indoor life completely, learned immediately (maybe from the other cats) what that "sand box" in the house was for, and never again showed even the slightest desire to go outside.

Often, strays have had enough of the outdoors. That's why they seek out human companionship. Generally, cats who were once strays accept life indoors fairly readily. It is as if they realize they have been given a second chance and are eager to take it. They have learned the hard way that the freedom of the outdoor life is not all it's cracked up to be, and they prefer the quiet life of a house cat, as long as their needs are met.

Snowball was left in my driveway, complete with carrier, one cold winter night. We took the extremely old and ill white cat in and nursed him back to health. Our assumption was that he had been an outdoor cat, perhaps even a stray. Yet he took to indoor life with no difficulty.

Still, it can be a challenge to acclimate a resident cat who has previously been allowed outdoors and in. Whether you adopt a previously outdoor cat who still wants out, or you wish to convert your resident outdoor cat to an indoor life, there are some steps you will need to take. This is a difficult situation for the cat, definitely a creature of habit. Restricting the movements of a cat who was once allowed to roam may sometimes be the genesis of what animal behaviorists call *confinement stress* (see chapter 3 for more on cats and stress). Suddenly being forced to stay inside is always quite a shock to a cat like this. The cat may become destructive, cry a lot, and try to escape every time a door is opened.

It may seem cruel to some people to try to keep a cat like this indoors, but it will really depend on you and the cat. You will need much patience and persistence, and a gentle, yet firm, manner.

For some cats, gradual acclimation to the indoors (bringing them in for longer and longer periods at a time) will work best. For others, being allowed outside even occasionally will only encourage the cat to want to go out more. In this case, it's best to bring the cat in and keep him there. If you live in an area with seasonal changes, the best time to do this is as winter approaches, when the cat will want to be inside more anyway.

---

### Online Resources

For more information and different views and techniques on teaching a cat to remain indoors, try the following sites:

www.geocities.com/
Heartland/Pointe/9352/
indoors.html

home.hiwaay.net/~keiper/
indoors.htm

www.pets.ca/pettips/
tips-29.htm

www.sdnhm.org/exhibits/
cats/indoors.html

www.maxshouse.com/
Healthy+Happy_
Indoors.htm

Distract the cat away from doors as best you can. Your cat will need an overabundance of love, attention, and distractions. Find out by experimentation which toys and games are your cat's favorites, and set up playtimes each day when the cat is at his most active. Try to re-create indoors the things your cat would normally be doing if he were to go outdoors (cat trees, cat grass, toy mice, ramps to run up, and so on). If all of your cat's desires are satisfied indoors, he will eventually find no need to go out and will settle into a quiet routine.

One word of warning here, though. A previously outdoor cat may never stop, at least on occasion, trying to slip outside. If possible, you might want to build an outdoor enclosure (see chapter 7) that will at least give your cat safe access to the outside and stop him from being interested in slipping out the door.

## Special Situations

After reading Gillie's story in the introduction, you shouldn't wonder why a previously outdoor cat might need to be brought indoors permanently. Sometimes situations arise in which this is the only practical solution. And amputation or illness are not the only reasons.

A cat who is extremely shy when you adopt him, even if he was previously an outdoor cat, may become frightened in a new situation and, when let outside, could get lost or disoriented.

There are people who are accident prone, and cats can be as well. Some cats just seem to find trouble wherever they go. A friend of mine once had a cat who, whenever he went outside, would come back scarred from a cat fight, mauled by a dog, or injured by a car. Eventually her only choice was to make him an indoor-only cat. If you have a cat who continually gets into fights with neighboring cats or other animals, it will probably be in the cat's best interest to keep him indoors.

A cat with a contagious or potentially deadly disease (such as feline leukemia virus) should also be kept in the house full time, for his own safety and the safety of other animals. A cat with a debilitating disease, or any illness that may affect his senses or responses (such as epilepsy), should be kept indoors for his own safety.

Blind or deaf cats do not have the necessary senses for dealing with the many dangers the outdoors has in store. If you adopt a blind cat or if an illness or injury blinds your cat, acclimating the cat to your home or to life indoors will require a little more effort than with a seeing cat. You might want to show the cat where everything is at first, by gently taking him on a tour of the house. Give him a space that is all his own—a space that's not too large—until he becomes accustomed to getting around.

Remember that your best tool is always patience when teaching any cat to live indoors, no matter what the animal's situation. Once both of you have adapted to each other, you can enjoy fun, games, and many years of indoor enjoyment together.

# 3

# Understanding
# Your Cat's Mind

**M**rs. Carter had always heard that when you're moving from one house to another, you should move the animals last. This way, she'd been told, the pet (in this case, her indoor-only Himalayan, Fluffer) would not feel so stressed as furniture and items were moved into the house. Nor did she have to worry about the cat slipping through an open door as the movers came in and out.

Mrs. Carter did everything as she had read in the cat book to do. The move was done, furniture in place. Personal possessions were still in boxes piled here and there, but the cat's items had been unpacked and set up in their proper locations: litter box in the bathroom, food and water dishes in the kitchen, even the cat tree had been placed by a big bay window in the den where the cat could bask in the daily sunshine. The last house had no den, so this would please Fluffer even more.

When it came time to bring Fluffer to her new home, Mrs. Carter was careful to speak reassuringly to her cat as she opened the carrier door. She sat with the cat on the plush carpeted floor, petting her and giving her treats to give the cat a positive experience in her new home. And Fluffer seemed to be doing just fine. Mrs. Carter followed the cat as the feline sniffed out each room. She made sure her beloved pet knew where the litter box was, and the cat tree and food and water as well. No problems at all, or so she thought.

During the following week, as she unpacked boxes, hung pictures and rearranged items, Mrs. Carter started to notice a difference in Fluffer's behavior. The normally playful and cuddly feline was mopey at some times, and seemed downright antisocial at others. The cat avoided her previously beloved cat tree completely. She tried cuddling with her cat, speaking to her, telling her everything would be all right—and she hoped the cat would snap out of whatever was troubling her. Finally, she took the cat to the vet, and there her pet's new doctor asked the vital question: Did other cats live in that house before you?

Mrs. Carter later discovered the previous owner did indeed have cats. One was a tomcat who had sprayed on the carpet in the den. The carpet had been cleaned so that human noses couldn't detect any odor. Fluffer, however, could. Everywhere the cat went, her sensitive nose picked up the scent of the previous owner's cats. To put it simply, Fluffer felt she was on another cat's turf—and she couldn't escape. Fluffer did not have a behavioral problem. She was just being a cat.

## When a Cat Is Just Being a Cat

Physically, a cat is much healthier when she stays indoors. But what about the cat's emotional health? Every cat has moments of stress, whether severe or slight, temporary or permanent. Stress is a natural part of existence, both human and animal. But in certain situations, the stress of confinement can cause behavioral problems and weaken the cat's immune system, making her more susceptible to disease.

To prevent, reduce, or eliminate stress, it helps to know why cats react as they do; what innate behaviors are responsible for their actions, likes, and dislikes?

Your cat's development and socialization began with Momma. Through contact and observation with her mother and siblings, then with humans and other cats, a kitten learns important behaviors that will shape her personality as an adult. This includes not only eating, hunting, grooming, litter box habits, playing, and scratching, but also socialization, fear, and aggression. Kittens with little or no human contact in their first four to seven weeks of life often never fully trust humans. Kittens raised only by humans often never develop proper skills of socialization when dealing with other cats. All these factors play a part in a cat's personality and tolerance for stress.

Certain types of aggression (such as mock play between kittens, which prepares them for dealing with other cats later in life), defending territory, and scratching are examples of behaviors that are normal for a cat but can be undesirable to her human owners. When these behaviors become a problem in the household (urinating outside the litter box, scratching the couch, or becoming suddenly aggressive, for example), often the underlying cause is a physical problem or stress. It's kitty's way of saying, "I need help."

If your cat is showing signs of stress-related behavior, the first step in solving the problem is taking the time to find out what is bothering her and why. Is your cat stressed because she was only recently converted to an indoor cat? Cats adjust well to indoor life if they have the proper essentials to fill their needs. But a cat who has lived most or all of her life outdoors and is now confined indoors may show more stress-related behavior than a cat who has never seen the outdoors.

Is your longtime house cat suddenly showing signs of stress? With an indoor cat, the signs of stress are more apparent than in the outdoor cat—particularly if they are displayed in a destructive manner—and you can work with your cat to do something about them. Ask yourself some questions and try to pinpoint the cause. What has changed in your life or your cat's? Has the cat been ill? Have you recently acquired a new pet? A baby? A spouse? New furniture? New cat litter?

Cats are intuitive and pick up on the emotions of others around them. Many times we will unknowingly create stress for our cats because of the stress in our own lives. Cats are proven stress-reducers for humans, lowering blood pressure and calming the nerves. But at times, in our effort to use our cats to alleviate our stress, we actually transfer the stress to them.

## Stress and Its Causes

Cats are creatures of habit and love their routine. Some cats adjust more readily to changes than others, but even the most independent and sedate cat will experience some stress when something in her life has changed. Stressful change can be physical, emotional, or environmental. To combat any of these stressors, you first must recognize the cause and then treat it appropriately, with patience and perseverance.

Let's take a closer look at some of the more common stressors that affect a house cat. Later in this chapter, I'll explain how you can help your indoor cat combat problems due to stress.

## Feline Rivalry

In my house, Pounce, Sammy, and Shadow love one another. They rarely if ever quarrel or even spat. Rather, they groom each other each

---

### Causes of Stress

| Physical | Emotional | Environmental |
|----------|-----------|---------------|
| Showing | Jealousy | Moving |
| Breeding | Death (human or | Crowding |
| Illness or injury | animal) | New animal or |
| Parasites | Separation or divorce | human family |
| Surgery | Feline rivalry | member |
| Obesity | Boredom, loneliness | Confinement |
| | Competition for | Loud noise |
| | affection | Lack of fresh air |
| | | and sunshine |

*In an ideal situation, cats in the same
household will groom one another.*

night, eat together, and know their place in one another's lives. This is an ideal situation, but it's not always the case in a multicat household. And the more cats in a household of indoor cats, the higher the incidence of stress and the greater the possibility of feline rivalry and aggression.

Although cats living in a multicat household will establish a pecking order, often forming little groups, close proximity can cause tempers to flare and the fur to fly. Even in households with only two or three cats who generally get along, there will be the occasional spat. In my household some of the cats have formed small social groups, while others prefer to remain solitary. Cats who are closest in age or were raised together are usually the ones who will get along the best. They form a hierarchy within their own little group and display behaviors that indicate the true nature of the domestic cat as a social animal: mutual grooming, and sleeping and playing together. (Cats are rumored to be solitary creatures, but anyone who lives with multiple cats or who has seen the boredom and behavioral problems of cats who do not receive enough social interaction, human or animal, knows otherwise.)

Social structures can also shift as time goes by. Cats, as they age, may grow apart and no longer share activities the way they once did. Taffy and Candy were a good example of this. Raised together as kittens, they once shared everything: sleeping space, food, playtime. Later in life, however, they barely tolerated each other. They would hiss, spit, and swat at each other if one wandered too close. No specific event or change triggered this; rather, it came about gradually as the cats aged and more cats arrived, shifting the social structure of the household.

Arguments in a cat society where two or more cats share the turf is normal, even necessary, to settle disagreements and establish a hierarchy. As normal as this behavior is, however, stress can still result, particularly when a cat from a group is bullying one of the solitary cats. Usually disagreements are settled on their own, with one of the cats walking away with little more than a scratch on the nose. But not always.

Feline rivalry, whether a harmless quarrel or an outright fight, can be caused by many factors. Let's take a look at the most common ones.

## Territorial Issues

Territorial disputes are a common problem in multicat households. If a new cat comes into the house, often the social structure will shift, causing a temporary disruption in the hierarchy. Introducing a cat should be done carefully, as outlined in chapter 2. Simply throwing new cats together is an invitation for trouble. They may eventually work it out, but why start out badly and cause more stress for your cats?

Any threat to a dominant cat's territory, even from a close companion, can cause disagreements. It's common to see spats over places in bed with you, sleeping rights for the comfy chair, a spot on the couch, and so on. Cats generally sort these disagreements out themselves without much problem.

If you feed strays or if unfamiliar cats come into your yard, occasionally this will also upset the cats in your house. Because they can't get at the outside intruders, they may quarrel with one another, sometimes viciously, or even with you. This is called displaced aggression. If you really must feed strays near your home (getting them to a shelter would be a better option), feed them out of sight of your indoor cats.

## Personality Clashes

Misinterpretation of intent causes spats, as well. As much as cats enjoy mutual grooming and playing, even this can turn into a disagreement. I have often seen this with my cats. One will be grooming the other, or they will be playing nicely, but one will decide she has had enough. If the other continues, a brief tiff ensues until one

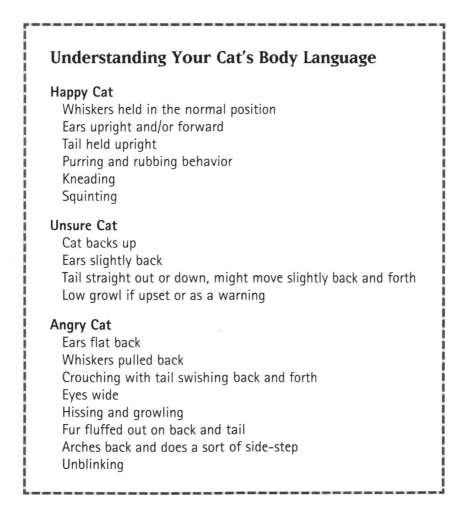

### Understanding Your Cat's Body Language

**Happy Cat**
  Whiskers held in the normal position
  Ears upright and/or forward
  Tail held upright
  Purring and rubbing behavior
  Kneading
  Squinting

**Unsure Cat**
  Cat backs up
  Ears slightly back
  Tail straight out or down, might move slightly back and forth
  Low growl if upset or as a warning

**Angry Cat**
  Ears flat back
  Whiskers pulled back
  Crouching with tail swishing back and forth
  Eyes wide
  Hissing and growling
  Fur fluffed out on back and tail
  Arches back and does a sort of side-step
  Unblinking

gives in and walks away. This type of argument generally flares up and is over quickly, with no harm done to either cat.

Sometimes cats simply do not get along. Personality clashes are common in multicat households, particularly where there are three or more cats. Some cats are just bullies. A cat considered lower in the pecking order by another cat may be bullied relentlessly by the stronger, more-assertive cat and may even have to be separated, either temporarily or permanently, from the pack. In addition, any change in household routine can upset the balance of the cats' hierarchy and raise stress levels, which may make cats more testy with one another—particularly if one or more of the cats doesn't tolerate stress well.

## Competition

Competition for food is a common cause of feline rivalry in a multicat household. Ensuring that each cat has her own food dish will not always solve this. Some cats simply want to eat from the other cat's dish and will sometimes even pull the dish away with a swift paw.

Competing for your attention and possession of toys can also cause the occasional spat; one cat wants what the other has.

## Scent

Scent can bring back a strong memory for a person, so just think what it must be like for your cat, whose sense of smell is so much greater than our own. Scent is also the primary way cats know and understand their world—including the other creatures in it.

A cat who has recently been outside, say to the veterinarian, will come home carrying a different scent. This can sometimes temporarily confuse the other cats in the household, who might even think the returning cat is a newcomer. Usually this is only a temporary problem and will resolve itself in a day or two as the home scent once again returns to the cat. But if the scent of an unfamiliar cat suddenly appears, or if the cat is moved to an unfamiliar location with strange odors (as in the story at the beginning of this chapter), your previously well-behaved puss might start to act different, or begin exhibiting territorial behavior (such as urinating in areas outside the litter box, on the bed, on the sofa, or even on clothing).

## Restoring Peace

So what can you do to solve disputes among your cats? If the problem only occurs at certain times or during certain activities, then a temporary "time out" or separating the cats at that time may help. For instance, if the cats fight over food or one cat steals from another, you may want to separate the more-dominant cat just during meals. This can mean feeding the cat in a separate area of the kitchen or in another room altogether.

Sometimes it's necessary to simply let the cats work out the differences on their own. If it's just a quick little spat and no one is getting hurt, don't worry. Allow the cats their space and they will quickly solve their differences.

Separate cat trees or trees with multiple levels will help solve disputes over the best spot to sleep or bask or simply view the world. Most cats will choose a favorite place to snooze, and providing enough places per cat should ensure the top cat stays on top, therefore calming territorial disputes.

If two cats are fighting relentlessly, or one cat bullies another, sometimes a quick squirt with water will separate the fighting cats. But this usually will not prevent future problems. Some people who have the room to do it separate the fighting cats permanently as an alternative to getting rid of one of the cats. My cat Shadow was fine as a kitten, but as he grew into adulthood he began bullying my oldest female, Taffy, to the point where she would rarely come out of hiding. To solve this, I set up a room for Taffy, away from Shadow, with her food, water, litter box, and sleeping area. I took her out so that she could sleep and play in the bay window during the day and sleep with me on my bed at night. A year later, I started keeping the door open, and she could come and go as she pleased. Shadow had learned he was not allowed in "Taffy's room," and she felt more secure knowing there was a special place she could go if he began bullying her.

*Herbs and Medicines*

Some people have used homeopathic medicines and flower remedies to alter their cat's behavior and calm frightened or belligerent attitudes. Some shelters use these remedies to calm feral cats and newcomers to the shelter. Bach Flower Essences Rescue Remedy is the original flower remedy, and is available at health food stores or by contacting the Dr Edward Bach Centre, Mount Vernon, Bakers Lane, Sotwell, Oxon, OX10 0PZ, UK; telephone: 44-0-1491-834678; fax: 44-0-1491 825022. Or visit the web site at www.bachcentre.com.

Although they should be used only in extreme cases and not permanently, certain antidepressants are also available to calm the nerves of a particularly stressed cat. These should only be given under the direct supervision of a veterinarian.

*Overcrowding*

Overcrowding among cats can cause a lot of arguments and territorial disputes. Moving to a larger house will give you and your cats more space, but this is not always a feasible solution. So if you can help it, don't bring more cats into the house than you can handle or your resident cats can get along with. Most experts recommend one cat per room of the house, but this depends on the size of the house, the size of the rooms, the personalities of the cats, and how much you can handle as far as care, feeding, attention, and vet bills.

Cats live in three dimensions, so one way to increase the amount of space in your home is by going vertical. More and/or taller cat trees will create more territory for each cat. So will perches hung on windowsills and bookshelves.

One of the best stress reducers, for both you and your cats, is play. Even cats who live with many other cats benefit from interaction and play with their owners—particularly the cats who do not belong to any social group formed among the cats in your home. Cats respond very positively to love and attention. Take time out, for yourself and your cats, to play with them, pet them, and show them your love each and every day.

# Loneliness

The opposite of the feline rivalry problem is the only-cat syndrome. When Taffy was a kitten we also had another cat, Bobby. But Bobby, being an older outdoor cat, was hardly a suitable playmate for a feisty kitten. After several weeks, we started to notice a change in Taffy. She didn't play as often and was beginning to become lethargic. She tried to play with Bobby the few times he came into the house, but he would simply swat her away and she would slink downstairs to stare at the wood stove. She was lonely and needed a companion.

A little more than a month after we acquired Taffy, we got Candy. Being close in age and activity level, Taffy and Candy needed no introduction. Young kittens rarely fight, even when presented to one another on the spot. After a short acclimation period to the house, Candy was ready and willing to be Taffy's playmate and companion, and Taffy couldn't have been happier. Her activity level picked up, and Candy and Taffy became inseparable.

Some cats, such as my brother's cat, Zoie, prefer being the lone cat and will not accept another cat on their turf. But even such independent, solitary cats can get lonely and may begin to exhibit signs of stress. Cats in multicat households, particularly those outside the hierarchy of a group, can also get lonely. Usually these cats prefer human companionship. But if their human is away much of the time, the cat may become lonely and stressed.

Like Taffy, some lonely or bored cats will simply stop playing and mope around the house. Other cats may become destructive or aggressive. Often only cats will "attack" their owner in mock play, as if the owner were another cat. This is a cat's way of recognizing you as a member of the cat's pack. Since there are no other cats to play with, you are your cat's only source of interactive amusement. Usually this mock attack–play goes no further than the occasional incident and causes no harm. In itself this may not be a sign the cat is bored or lonely. Shadow, although he has many other cats in his pack who he plays with daily, still enjoys an occasional "battle" with my arm or a swipe at my legs as I walk by. There is no harm in this; he is recognizing me as another cat, which to a cat is quite an honor.

But with a lonely or bored cat this behavior can sometimes get out of hand. The cat may start to attack often or viciously, or become downright nasty. This kind of behavior should not be encouraged, particularly with children in the house. A cute young kitten's innocent scratches can become painful wounds (which may lead to infection) as the cat grows older and bigger.

What if you already have an only cat who will not accept another cat or kitten into the household, yet is beginning to show signs of boredom or loneliness? If you can, pay more attention to the cat. I know this sounds obvious, but I am still surprised at the number of people who don't pay enough attention to their cats. Because of the cat's independent nature, it seems as if they need no one. But nothing could be further from the truth.

If you are away much of the time (due to a job or something else that cannot be helped), make sure the cat has plenty of toys to play with that will keep her occupied throughout the day: cat trees to climb, greens to nibble, and windows to look out. Besides these, you

*Something as simple as a video or DVD might prove great entertainment for your cat while you're away.*

may want to try leaving the television or radio on when you are away. Soft music has been known to reduce stress and relax cats. There are even videos and DVDs available that you can play for your cat (*Video Catnip* and *Cat Sitter DVD* are two examples). Some of these show birds, squirrels, and wildlife scenes, which, the video makers assume, will entertain a cat. Watch your cat's reaction to these films and you'll know if they were right.

Some experts recommend obtaining a different kind of pet for your cat, such as fish. My cats would sit for hours on top of or beside the fish tanks, staring at and trying to catch the fish. Just make sure the tank has a secure lid, or the fish may become snacks rather than pets.

Small animals such as hamsters or gerbils won't be much use as companions for a cat. Although some cats may enjoy watching the tiny animal in its cage, the cat's presence will most likely scare the animal more than benefit the cat.

Ferrets, as mentioned in the previous chapter, are sometimes good companions for cats. However, be sure the two get along well, and even then it's not a great idea to leave them alone together when you're not home. Also, check the laws in your area; ferrets are illegal in some states.

Rats make great pets, don't bite, and are intelligent. Often if they are raised with a cat and introduced properly, the two can get along well (though I still would not recommend leaving them alone together). My rats no longer fear my cats, because the presence and scent of the cats is always there.

Be careful with dogs as well. Although some cats love dogs as companions (such as my cat Pounce) and they will get along great, some dogs will not appreciate a cat as a companion. Make sure they are getting along well before leaving them alone together. Some breeds of dogs are naturally better with cats than others, but almost any friendly dog can learn to accept a new pet cat.

If there is a tree outside your house (or a balcony, if you live in an apartment on a higher floor) you may want to place bird feeders where the cat can watch safely through a window or door as the birds come to visit (in a city this may be pigeons, but the cat doesn't care).

## Jealousy or a Change in Routine

A sudden change in a cat's behavior when a new person or pet comes into your home is more than likely a jealous reaction. Any change to a cat's comfortable position in the home that may take away the owner's attention can cause jealousy. Be aware, though, that "jealousy" is something we know humans feel, and can only suppose cats feel. What we do know for sure is that as circumstances change, stress ensues and the cat's behavior changes. Even a simple change, such as a shift in job hours or scheduling, can upset a cat's normal routine and cause stress.

I know a woman who got in the habit of playing with her cat every morning before she went to work. One morning she was running late and did not have time for the usual routine. She laid her work clothes out on the bed and went into the bathroom to get ready. When she came back into the bedroom to get dressed, she found the cat had left a "present" waiting for her right smack in the middle of her clothes.

Cats grow accustomed to the love and affection they receive from their owners. Living with a cat has often been likened to raising a child, and for good reason. Cats thrive on love, attention, and security as much as a child does. Jealousy is a powerful emotion, and when an event occurs that interferes with a cat's comfortable routine, often insecurity will result and the cat will show her disapproval the only way she knows how. Usually this means inappropriate behavior, such as urinating or defecating outside the litter box or scratching where she is not supposed to scratch (this behavior is not to be confused with a cat who simply has not yet learned the proper place to scratch). Those are the most common behaviors a jealous cat will exhibit, but other signs can also indicate a cat is unhappy about something. Some cats will go off their food, mope, stop grooming themselves, or become destructive.

A new baby in the house is a common cause of jealousy in house cats, especially if the cat is accustomed to regular attention from her owner. A cat does not understand why this tiny, wailing person is taking up all her owner's attention. A cat who has a companion she spends much of her time with (preferably another cat) will probably not be as affected by this change as a cat whose owner is her whole world, but even in a two-cat family, more attention from the owner can mean the difference between upset and comfort.

A new spouse or another pet in the house can also upset a cat's world. During a time of change, a cat may feel her security and place in the household are threatened. But you want your cat to be accepting, not put off, by the new addition to your house. Thus, you'll need to work extra hard to maintain your cat's regular routine. The cat will also need even more attention than she usually gets. This special attention gives your cat something to take pleasure in as well, and will remind her that nothing has changed in your heart and that she has nothing to fear.

## Death or Divorce

At one time, Pounce used to sit side by side with my stepfather Ray's Husky, Orion, taking cheese from Ray as he made his sandwiches for work. As the dog got older and became less and less mobile, Pounce would wait for Orion, or even go and fetch him so they could share their cheese together. When Orion died, Pounce was lost. He moped around the house for weeks and refused cheese for more than a year after that.

Cats are extremely sensitive creatures. There is no question that they feel grief at the loss of a loved one—animal or human. And they often experience in silence their pains and those of their caretaker.

When something has happened to upset a cat's person, often the cat, too, will feel upset. This puts stress on the cat, and as hard as it may be when you are feeling bad, the cat will require extra attention and love to get through this stressful period. Your cat can help you, as well. Remember, the love and attention you lavish on your cat during a difficult time is good for you both. The act of petting a cat has been scientifically proven to reduce stress, alleviate depression, and lower blood pressure in humans—and cats. During low periods you need your cat just as much as your cat needs you, and this is a good time to sit in quiet contemplation with your cat in your lap, relaxing.

# Signs of Stress

Each cat is an individual and will show stress in her own way. Destructive behavior is one sign I've already mentioned, and there are many others. It's important to recognize that these are stress behaviors and are not simply your cat acting willful or naughty. Then the trick is to find out why your cat is stressed and address the problem.

Remember, too, that whenever you see a change in your cat's behavior, it is important to first rule out any physical ailment. That means a thorough checkup by the veterinarian. If the cat receives a clean bill of health from your veterinarian and obvious stressors are not apparent (or are eliminated) but the cat is still exhibiting a change in behavior, then you will have to do a little detective work. Your cat cannot tell you if she is feeling down, but she will show you.

## Refusing to Use the Litter Box

This is the most common way cats exhibit their stress. Many times the stress stems from too many cats sharing a litter box, competition from other cats, or another cat picking on the affected cat and thus causing her to fear going to the box. Giving this cat her own box may help.

This problem can also stem from a previous physical illness, such as a urinary disorder or bowel problem. A cat with a urinary or bowel problem may find it painful to urinate or defecate, and thus associate the pain with using the litter box and begin to avoid it. Even after the illness has been successfully treated, the cat may still be afraid of using the box. If this is the case, carefully retraining the cat may be required.

Other litter box factors that can stress a cat include the brand of litter used, how clean the box is, the location and size of the box, the use of litter liners, and the number of boxes per cat. See chapter 4 for complete litter box information.

A recently declawed cat may not want to use the box, as the litter can hurt her sensitive feet. Temporarily replacing the litter with a softer substance (such as sawdust, sand, or shredded paper) can help (see chapter 5 for more on the issue of declawing).

If your cat is 6 months old or older and is not yet altered, you may be seeing signs of a cat's natural tendency to mark territory. Cats are territorial, and urination is an innate behavior that both males and females use to mark boundaries. Cats who are altered before sexual maturation are less likely to develop this habit.

Senior cats may have more difficulty holding their urine. A trip to the vet may be in order, as he or she may be able to prescribe a medication to help your cat. Your veterinarian may also recommend certain tranquilizers or medications to help modify an inappropriate behavior such as indiscriminate urination.

## Overgrooming

Often, when a cat feels stressed, she will take her frustrations out on herself, either by excessive licking or overgrooming. Some cats will overgroom to the point of creating bald patches or open sores on their skin.

## Loss of Coat Condition

A cat's coat is a good indication of her well-being. If a cat is ill or under excessive stress, her coat will shed more heavily and become dry and dull. She may groom excessively or not groom at all. Often a cat's skin will flake and the fur will shed when the cat gets nervous or upset. If you've ever taken your cat to the veterinarian and ended up almost as furry as the cat, you already know about this.

## Listlessness

A normally active cat, when under stress, might become listless and mope around the house, actually acting depressed. Many times a cat will refuse to play—even her favorite games. Listlessness is common in cats who have recently experienced the death of a person or pet close to them, but any one of the stressors listed in this chapter can produce this response.

## Changes in Eating Habits

This can include anything from the cat refusing to eat at all to eating more than usual. If your cat refuses to eat and a physical exam has ruled out any possibility of illness or dental problems, then finding the cause of the cat's stress is imperative. Talk to your veterinarian about the best course of action to get your cat eating properly (see chapter 10 for more information on diet for the indoor cat).

## Chewing

A cat who suddenly begins eating your plants or develops a taste for inedible objects (such as a blanket or your clothes) may be showing a stress-related behavior. She may also have a medical problem, so be sure to have her checked by your veterinarian.

## Aggression

This may include aggression toward other cats or people. A cat under stress may begin to bite, claw, and growl at other cats for no apparent reason. While I mentioned earlier that little cat spats are nothing to worry about, aggression from stress is different from other types of normal feline aggression, such as playful aggression (when two cats or kittens are mock-fighting, there will be little or no growling and claws will not be fully extended) or petting aggression (some cats will only tolerate being petted for so long, then will bite or claw at your hand to let you know they have had enough). Some cats, particularly feral cats or cats who lack proper socialization, will be aggressive to some extent as part of their personality.

Aggression is a sign of stress only if it comes on suddenly or is the result of a change in the cat's life. Aggression can also be a sign that something physical is wrong. Often when a cat does not feel well, she will show her discomfort by aggressively protecting the area that hurts. A trip to the vet can rule out a physical ailment.

## Displaced Aggression

Dogs and wolves are not the only animals to form hierarchies. In a multicat household, the cats also establish a pecking order that tells each cat in the household who's on what level in the group. This is true even when you have just two cats.

If a higher-ranking cat is picking on a lesser cat, many times the lesser cat will take her frustration out on a cat even lower in the hierarchy. This is called displaced or redirected aggression. It frequently occurs when a new cat is brought into the household and temporarily upsets the established order, and generally works itself out over time. But if you're seeing displaced aggression in a well-established group, you need to find out exactly what the problem is.

## Fear

Any of the stressors mentioned in this chapter can cause a fear reaction in a cat. Fear itself can also cause stress. A fearful cat will display any number of the signs of stress already mentioned.

Often a fearful cat will show aggression toward another cat, or even her owner. A frightened cat will hide and, if forced to come out, will show her reluctance by attacking. Displaced aggression can result with lesser cats in the pecking order, who may grow fearful if the top cat is bullying or intimidating.

Calming the fearful cat will require patience and understanding. In severe cases, a feline behaviorist can be called in to help solve the problem (as well as other behavioral problems and stressors). Speak with your veterinarian about possible

 **Online Resources**

For more on behavioral consultation or to find a cat behavior therapist, you can try the following:

www.vetmedicine.about
.com/cs/catdiseasesb/a/
catbehavior.htm

www.meowhoo.com/
Behavior_Training/Cat_
Behavior_Consultants

www.littlebigcat.com

www.catsinternational.org

medications and treatments to calm the cat's nerves, as well. But remember that medication is, at best, a short-term solution; directly addressing your cat's fear and stress is the long-term answer.

## Stress Relievers

When you see signs of stress, you must find and eliminate the specific cause. There are also other steps you can take to prevent or lessen your cat's general stress level.

### Good Nutrition

It is vital that all cats be fed a good diet that is 100 percent nutritionally complete for cats (see chapter 10 for more on diet). When stress levels are elevated, a proper diet that is supplemented with veterinarian-recommended vitamins may help to reduce the physical effects of stress in your cat.

### Exercise

During stressful times, as with humans, a cat may be lethargic or less active. Exercise is a proven stress reliever, so during stressful times

*Keep your cat's weight down with play and exercise.*

*Cats need to play to avoid boredom.*

add some extra playtime with your cat. Regular exercise also helps prevent stress from building up under normal circumstances.

Exercise also helps keep the cat's weight down (obesity may stress the cat's body, thus making the cat more lethargic and vulnerable to further stress). Cats love to chase objects. Throwing a ball for your cat is a good form of exercise—for yourself as well as your cat, because cats seldom fetch. Pounce loves to chase balls and, unlike most cats, will even bring them back if the ball is spongy enough for him to grip in his mouth.

## Companionship

One cat or two? Two cats will be twice the trouble, right? Not necessarily. Two cats, particularly kittens or adult cats who know each other and are proven to get along, will not only take some of the burden off you, but will also prevent some types of stress. There will be an added vet bill, and the litter box will need cleaning a bit more often, but the benefits for the cats will far outweigh the negatives.

Obtaining two cats will also help prevent an only cat from developing king-of-the-house syndrome, which can occur when a cat is raised alone. Dominant cats see a need to keep peace in their community, and once another cat breaks the boundaries, trouble can ensue. A cat who grows from kittenhood to adulthood alone often will not tolerate another cat being brought in later on.

Two cats raised together will have each other for company. They will play together and sleep together, even groom each other. This leaves you a little more freedom to go out more often and not feel guilty about the cat being home alone.

However, this does not mean the cats will need nothing from you. Cats love their humans, and even with other cats to play with, they still require and thrive on love from the person who cares for them. The relationship between two cats is a very different one from the relationship between cat and human, and both are beneficial not only to the cats but to you.

## Space

Cats don't require as much space as some pets, but they still need some room to run and play. Crowding among cats can also cause stress, so be sure you have enough room to meet each cat's individual needs. Also, do not have more cats than your home can fit or that you can properly care for.

## Communication

Good communication between you and your cat is essential so you will know when something is amiss. Know your cat's body language and usual activity level, what toys are her favorites, and how she normally behaves when she's happy. That way, you'll know when something is not right. Communicating with your cat also helps form a bond between you that can help to reduce stress for the cat as well as for yourself.

## Attention and Love

Never underestimate the healing power of love. Provide your cat with plenty of attention, toys, games, and TLC. Try to set aside a specific time every day to hold, pet, and play with your cat (or each cat in

*Two kittens are better than one and will keep each other company.*

your care). Even if your cat seems shy, she needs attention (maybe even more so). Spend time with her and let her come out of her shell through your loving care.

Talk to your cat every day. Look right at her when you do—she'll love the attention. Don't be afraid to use baby talk with your cat. Cats particularly enjoy soft voices. Whenever I baby-talk my cats, they begin to purr and squint their eyes, a sign of contentment. They sense and know I love them. They can feel it and they respond accordingly.

## Interaction, Toys and Games

My cat Pounce has a simple rule concerning play: If it moves, pounce on it. If it doesn't move, make it move, then pounce on it.

Cats need to interact and play. Many cats, such as Pounce, make their own games and their own fun. Others need to be enticed. Catnip, bird feeders outside the windows, scratching trees, toys, and kitty greens are all essential elements to an indoor cat's well-being.

Be careful which toys you choose for your cat. Simply because a toy is offered for sale does not guarantee it is safe for your cat. Knowing your cat is the first rule in knowing which are the best toys to provide for her entertainment. If your cat is an avid chewer (kittens often fall into this category), try to avoid toys that have string,

*Find toys your cat or kitten likes best.*

wire, or small pieces that can come off and get lodged in the cat's throat or digestive tract.

Make up games and experiment until you find the ones your cat enjoys most, then set aside time each day to play these games. Some cats will enjoy obstacle courses to run, soap bubbles to chase, or just a rolled up ball of foil to bat around. Interactive toys, such as a feather or toy mouse on a string and fishing pole–type toys, are fabulous for keeping a cat's mind and muscles toned. When Shadow was younger (and smaller), he would run up me as if I were a tree and perch on my shoulder. This was a game he developed on his own. So watch your cat and see what kind of games she enjoys.

Some pet supply stores sell toys that don't even require your involvement. These toys run on batteries and consist of a plastic base (generally shaped like a cat or even a mouse) and a long thin shaft on which a stringed toy is attached. The base has a motor inside that spins the shaft in different directions, enticing your cat to chase the small mouse or tuft on the end of the string. These toys are fine for a little while, but most cats tire of them pretty quickly because they are too predictable. There is really no substitute for interactive play with you.

## Cat Agility

The sport of agility has long been a favorite with dog owners. Dogs navigate an obstacle course, with their owners at their side, using up excess energy, challenging their mind, and having a great time. This sport is now becoming more and more popular among cat owners as well, as a form of recreation and exercise for their cats. If you want to enter the competitions, you need to start training when your cat is young and get her used to traveling to matches. But almost any cat who does not get terribly stressed about going places can try out this new and innovative sport. And the best part is that you can train your cat right at home and put her through the obstacle courses for fun, or get together with friends. There is a form of cat agility for almost anyone. For more information, check out www.catagility.com.

Try not to get your cat into the habit of playing with your hands. This can cause the cat to associate scratching and biting hands with play and enjoyment.

## Massage

Who doesn't love a good massage? Cats do, too! Cats can benefit from massage, not only for its stress-relieving qualities, but also because a massage gives you the chance to check your cat for any lumps, scabs, or physical abnormalities.

Most cats will readily accept a massage, as long as it is done when the cat is in the mood to be petted and rubbed. A cat will usually let you know when she has had enough by getting vocal, suddenly scratching (as some cats will do), or simply walking away.

Giving a cat a massage involves a little more than a simple petting. Using your thumbs, carefully rub the cat, starting with her head, in light, slow, circular motions. Massaging at the animal's muscles, work your way down to the neck, back, legs, and paws. Some cats will

*A good massage can be really relaxing!*

enjoy it so much they may roll over for you to rub their belly. Just as with petting, massage will relieve your own stress as well as your cat's.

## Catnip

We all know the effects catnip can have on our cats. A member of the mint family, catnip relaxes cats and gives them a safe, nonaddictive buzz. The chemical responsible for this reaction is called nepetalactone, and it works through the cat's sense of smell. The scent stimulates certain nerves in the cat's brain, resulting in a cat who is relaxed enough to either get crazy or sleep soundly (or sometimes both), depending on the cat. Not all cats are affected by catnip, however, and young kittens rarely are.

## Music

You have heard that music can soothe the savage beast. It can soothe your domestic cat as well. Soft, classical music or even a radio playing very low can keep your cat(s) company and help relax them when you are not home. Avoid heavy, driving, loud music. You might love it, but a cat's sensitive ears will not. Also, remember to keep the radio or television on low volume. If you can just barely hear it, your cat will hear it at just the right level.

## Special Situations

Some cats have physical limitations such as illness, blindness, deafness, or a crippling deformity. These cats may experience a higher level of stress due to their handicap. Cats such as these need special care and love. However, conventional stress-reduction methods may not work as well with these cats, so alternative methods must be developed to ease and reduce any stress.

Gillie, the three-legged cat, used to play lying down a lot. He would roll onto his back and hold a catnip toy between his front paws, making his own games. One day he discovered that toy balls were extremely fun. Pounce had rolled one that stopped right in front of Gillie as he sat there, watching. Being an outdoor cat most of his life, I don't think he knew what a toy ball was. He tried touching it and was absolutely amazed when it moved. His eyes went wide. He touched it again, a bit harder, and it rolled a couple of inches. That's when it dawned on him: the harder it's touched, the farther it rolls. From then on (and even the night he died), he loved to chase those toy balls.

If you have a special-situation cat, get to know what things the cat will respond to and use that knowledge to create play events for your particular cat. With plenty of fun activity and love, your cat should feel less stressed and will live a longer and happier life.

# The Cat-Friendly Home

Obviously, owning a cat will mean certain changes in your home: cat trees adorning the living room, fancy sofas covered by towels, and cat beds and toys blanketing the floor. Besides these basics, there are other things you can do to make your home fun and friendly for your cat. Remember, you are creating your cat's entire world. With a little thought and ingenuity, that world can be heaven for your cats. The following are just a few fun ideas that will make your home more cat friendly.

What is it cats like to do (besides eating, scratching, and sleeping)? They play, hide, and climb. Cats prefer a high vantage point from which to view their domain. Sure, your cats have that wonderful tall cat tree to sit on top of, but that's only one vantage point. Rather than placing a huge cat tree in every room, ramps and perches can be made using a little imagination and skill.

Wooden ramps can be built that lead up walls or onto the counter. Does your cat like to sit on top of the refrigerator? Stairs or a ramp built on the side of the fridge make a wonderful and fun way for your cat to get to one of her favorite spots. Carpeting these ramps not only gives the cat a good grip, but provides an extra scratching area, as well. These ramps can be built along walls in any room or in only one room. I've seen ramps that run from one room to the next. A hole

## Keep Kitty Happy

- Give her a place to use her claws, stretch, and climb.
- Lots of attention, petting, and TLC goes a long way.
- Toys, toys, toys.
- A nice, sunshiny window to sleep in.
- Cat greens to munch on are always fun.
- Cleanliness rules where cats are concerned. Keep that litter box clean!
- Keep food and water away from litter. Do you eat dinner in the bathroom?
- Always provide fresh, clean water!
- Each cat should have their own spaces to relax away from anyone else if they choose.
- Can your kitty see what's going on outside? Cats love to watch the neighborhood happenings.

in the wall makes it easy for the cat to get from one room to another without ever having to touch the floor. The choice is yours, and the type of ramps you build and where you place them are limited only by your imagination.

Cabinets are great places for little furry bodies to hide, but you don't want your cat getting into the cabinets that house your cleaning supplies and chemicals. A box or cabinet can be constructed specifically for your cat using either cardboard or wood. (If wood is used, be careful with nails. It's better to use a nontoxic glue.)

I once built a kitty castle using several durable cardboard boxes. I cut cat-size holes in various places in each box, then strategically glued them together so that one box led to the next. I painted the whole house and placed towels in the bottom of each box. I even built a little open courtyard on one side. If you use sturdy-enough cardboard, you can even carpet the whole thing. To attract the cats to it, I attached toys on strings and hung them outside the doors, then placed more toys inside.

## The Kitty Stampede

It's the middle of the night when suddenly . . . a herd of elephants comes charging down the stairs. Or so it seems. Cats love to run, and it will be in your cat's best interest as well as your valuables if you provide space for them to do so. If you have a hallway, great, but my cats prefer the stairs. Wherever your cat likes to run, make sure the way is clear and free of anything breakable.

# 4

# Bathroom Duty

The cat was about to climb into the litter box when his caretaker noticed him back away and move out of the room. The person couldn't smell anything, but the cat could. He decided the carpet was much more sanitary to use as a bathroom than a litter box that had not been cleaned in several days.

I know it's a nasty job, and many cat owners have told me the reason they don't keep their cats indoors is because they dread even the thought of cleaning litter boxes. But is avoiding litter box duty worth the risk of allowing your cat outside? Besides, today there are so many innovations in litter and litter boxes that cleaning them is barely a task at all.

First, let's talk about your relationship with your cat. Your indoor cat relies on *you*. He no longer has all of outdoors to choose as a bathroom, so it's *your* duty to provide a place that will satisfy his instincts and enable him to continue to go where nature has preprogrammed him to feel most comfortable going.

*You* are the one who must decide where the litter box is placed, what type of litter to use, what kind of litter box is best for your cat(s), how many boxes you should have, and what to do if your cat stops using the litter box. *You* are the one who must scoop and clean

*Would you want to step in a litter box that looks like this?*

the box regularly. But if you make all the decisions based on what you want and ignore what your cat wants and needs, *he* will be the one who chooses where *he* wants to go!

## Litter Box Fillers

Before it was widely known that cats could survive happily indoors, most cats never even saw a litter box. The rare times when they were kept indoors, due to bad weather or some other temporary problem, they had to make do with a box, usually wooden, filled with sand or ash. These fillers did little to neutralize odors and were not always the most absorbent or easily cleaned materials.

But in 1947 an event occurred that changed the feline world: Kitty Litter, the first publicly marketed cat-box filler, was discovered quite by accident. Edward Lowe, who at the time worked for his father's industrial supply company, was visited by his neighbor, who asked him if he had any sand she could use for her cat's box. The weather was cold and the sand Lowe had outside was frozen, so he gave her a bag of granulated clay to try. She used the clay and then remarked to Lowe how it was wonderfully absorbent and easy to clean. This gave Lowe an idea. He filled some bags with the clay, called them Kitty Litter and marketed his product, first locally and then at cat shows around the country. Kitty Litter was a huge success.

Since 1947 hundreds of different types and brands of cat-box filler have been marketed. Go to any pet supply or grocery store and you will be faced with a bewildering variety of choices.

Just as every cat is different, so is every litter and every cat's litter preference. Cats are clean, picky creatures, and some cats will refuse to use certain litters for reasons that may or may not be obvious to you. But with the variety of litters available, you can always find one that your cat likes.

## Clay Litter

At one time, traditional clay litter was the only type available commercially, and the only odor-control ingredient used by cat owners was baking soda sprinkled on the top of the litter. Now clay litter is available in many different varieties, from unscented natural to ones that incorporate odor crystals and deodorants.

Clay litter is inexpensive and comes in many varieties, making it the most widely available cat litter on the market. The two drawbacks most often mentioned about clay litter is that it tends to be tracked around the house, and that the clay can be dusty, which may irritate some cats. Putting a carpet remnant at the entrance to the litter box can reduce tracking. Some companies now also sell mats that help clean litter off a cat's feet as he exits the box. Dust-free clay litters are available, too.

If you have only one or two cats, clay litter can be a great choice, particularly for someone on a limited budget. However, traditional clay litters are not always best for the multicat household. Even the ones with the most odor-absorbing compounds cannot always keep up in a household with several cats. And while solid wastes should be scooped from all litter boxes every day, traditional clay litters do not enable you to remove the urine without dumping all the litter. Therefore, the litter must be changed every three to five days, depending on the number of cats in your household.

## Clumping Clay Litter

Nine out of ten cats agree that clumping litter is the way to go. Developed around 1984 by a biochemist named Thomas Nelson, the biggest chunk of litter sales today are clumping litters. These litters are treated with chemicals that cause the clay to bond when moistened. The cat owner can then simply scoop the clump from the box, leaving no urine or odor behind.

Like traditional clay litters, the clumping varieties are available in many different types, including low dust, low tracking, multicat, deodorized, crystal blend, baking soda, natural, and many combinations of these. Clumping litters are great for households with many cats and enable you to remove all the waste quickly, including the urine.

The texture of clumping clay litters is more like sand than other forms of litters, and is therefore widely accepted by most cats. At one time the clumping litters were the priciest litters on the market, but today prices have gone down. Like anything, there are still quality varieties and generic, or less-expensive, varieties. I have found that the quality clumping litters cost only a dollar or two more but are well worth the extra money because the clumps don't fall apart as you are scooping them.

### Clumping Litter and Kittens

Awhile back, there was some controversy about whether clumping litters can form clumps in a cat's stomach and intestinal tract after the cat has licked it from his paws. It has since been determined that these litters are safe for adult cats, but are not recommend with kittens under 4 months of age. Usually the amount of litter left on a cat's paws after he steps from the box, walks across the floor, and then stops to clean himself is so small that no health problems result from an adult swallowing a bit of it. Dogs who have been known to snack from the litter box have also had no troubles.

Certain clumping litters (usually the cheaper varieties), if not scooped constantly, can form cementlike clumps that stick to the bottom of the box. These are difficult to remove after they have been allowed to build up. Or the clumps fall apart and end up back in the box when you scoop. When buying clumping litter, it is best to experiment and find the brand you and your cat prefer.

Tracking also seems to be a complaint about clumping litters, but now there are reduced-tracking litters available. These litters have a larger grain, which helps reduce the amount of litter trapped between a cat's toes.

Does removing the clumps mean you never have to dump the litter and replace it completely? No! Germs still stick to the litter box, so for your cat's health and the clean smell of your home, the box should be dumped and cleaned, and the litter replaced at least every few weeks.

## Crystal Litters

There are several different types of crystal litters, as well as many crystal litter blends. The crystals are silica, a porous substance that traps the urine and its odors. I admit these litters are a bit pricey, but most of them claim that one small bag will last a month with one cat. They also claim to be among the most powerful at absorbing odors.

The crystal litters' claim that they last longer than clay or clumping litters is generally made for households with one cat. In my experience, however, these are not the best litters for households with more than three cats.

There are also litters that combine clumping clay and crystals, and sometimes even baking soda (such as Arm & Hammer Crystal Blend Cat Litter). Personally, I like these litters the best. They provide the odor-absorbing qualities of the crystals with the convenience of the clumping litters. Plus, they are more comfortable on a cat's feet.

## Wood Litters and Pellets

Cedar and pine are the most common woods used for these types of litters. Litters with a cedar base are very odor absorbent, and wood litters are environmentally friendly. Although wood litters, particularly cedar, can be used well in multicat situations, like traditional clay they do not clump and need to be replaced and the box cleaned more often than with the clumping litters.

However, as with everything, new and innovative litters have been created from wood. Litters such as Feline Pine are environmentally friendly pellet litters made of pine, which naturally bonds with the ammonia from the urine, thus destroying odors. Pellets also do not track, are usually flushable, contain no chemicals, and claim to be among the healthiest cat litters to use.

However, some cats will not use pellet litters because they can be hard on the feet.

## Corncob and Corn Litters

Because corncob litter is made from a product that is normally considered food, most people don't think of it as suitable for a litter box—might the cats eat it instead? But companies that manufacture corncob litters claim it is milled in a way that makes it unappealing to the palate. And if cats were to eat it, the litter would simply pass through their digestive tract with no difficulty.

Corncob litter is milled by separating the cobs into two parts, light and heavy. The parts are then ground up, heated, and made into pellets, which are then ground again and put through a filtering process. Besides being biodegradable, clumpable, flushable, and virtually dust free, corncob litters are highly absorbent and appealing to most cats.

A fairly recent addition to the list of available cat litters is made from whole-kernel corn. It is a clumping litter that is easy on a cat's feet. There are no fragrances, oils, or perfumes and the litter is flushable and biodegradable. I have not had the chance to try this litter yet because it is not widely available, but you can find it at Petsmart or through its Web site at www.petsmart.com.

## Newspaper

While shredded newspaper is sometimes recommended for cats immediately after declawing, it is not suitable for long-term litter box use. Instead, there is a litter for the eco-conscious person made from recycled newspaper. This litter is put through a process that binds the ink so it will not come off on the cat's paws or be tracked through your house. In small quantities, this litter is flushable and absorbent.

This litter is soft and lightweight and therefore more gentle on sensitive feet, so if your cat has recently had surgery (particularly declawing or other surgeries involving the feet), this might be a good choice.

### Grass

Bales of straw and grasses are chopped up and ground into small pieces, which are then put through a pelleting process to manufacture these litters. The process prevents them from falling apart when moistened. Grass litter is eco-friendly and absorbent, and tends to control urine odors better than traditional clay litters. But, like other pelleted litters, they may not be friendly on the cat's feet.

### Citrus Peels, Grains, Wheat, and Peanut Shells

These litters are also eco-friendly. Citrus cat litters are made from recycled fruit wastes, generally the peels from dejuiced citrus fruits. They are cooked at a high temperature to kill off bacteria, and the dust is cleaned out through a filtering process. The residual acids on the fruit peels help to reduce and neutralize the ammonia smell in the cat's urine, almost completely eliminating odors.

Grain and wheat litters are made in much the same way as pet foods. Gluten in grain litters helps make them clumpable. These litters are also flushable and can actually be good for a septic system by adding enzymes. Peanut shell litter, grain litter, and wheat litter are all edible, as well. So if kitty decides to make a snack out of his litter, there will be no harmful effects.

## Making Your Choice

So many choices can make buying litter confusing. But the upside is that there is enough variety to ensure that every cat will be happy.

Sometimes litters can be mixed to offer you the advantages of one litter and your cat the advantages of another. My cats, for instance, prefer the clumping litters, and I like the ease of cleaning them. But with some cats, the odor-controlling properties of one litter might not be enough (if you have many cats in the house, some might want one kind of litter, while others prefer something else). You can try experimenting by filling the box with one litter and placing a thin layer on top of a softer litter.

Your best bet is to experiment and find out which litter or combination of litters is most preferred by you and your cat(s). Your cat will let you know what he does and doesn't like. The most common way cats send this message is simply to refuse to use the box. Dissatisfied cats will often eliminate on the floor near the box.

## Litter Boxes

Of course, you need something to put the litter in. There are almost as many types and styles of litter boxes as there are litters. What kind of litter box is right for your cat? The answer will depend on your cat, your preference, the space available, and where the box (or boxes) will be placed.

For kittens, it is probably best to start out with a smaller, open box and get a larger one when the cat grows big enough for it. A large box for a small kitten is not a good idea. A kitten who continuously has to struggle to climb into the box may decide the effort is not worth it and start doing his business in other locations.

Many styles of boxes are designed with ease of cleaning in mind. Some companies sell boxes with one or more movable parts that sift the litter from one box to the next, with the solid waste then easily discarded. Although they can be used with almost any litter type, these litter boxes work best with clumping litters.

Some people (and some cats) prefer covered litter boxes. These give kitty a private place to go, help keep odors from spreading throughout the house, and keep litter spills to a minimum—a real concern if your cat likes to scratch a lot in the litter. Covered litter boxes now come in a variety of shapes, such as ones that can be placed in a corner, and most come with the latest in odor-eating filters.

## Do It Yourself

Sometimes you can be innovative and make your own litter box, rather than buying one from the store. This litter box was previously a cat bed no cat seemed to want to sleep in. Made of durable plastic and just the right size, the cats may not have wanted to sleep in it, but they have had no objection to using it as their bathroom.

While some cats prefer the privacy, others will not use a covered box. I am not sure if cats can be called claustrophobic, but some cats definitely have an aversion to stepping through a tiny hole to do their duty (these same cats may also hate the confines of a carrier, so perhaps they *are* claustrophobic).

If you choose to use a covered box and your cat accepts it, be sure you don't forget to scoop every day. Because the odors are kept within the box for the most part and the dirty litter is not as obvious as with an open box, it can be easy to forget that the box must be cleaned just as regularly. Many cats will not go in a dirty box and will let you know when the box is simply too dirty for them by leaving you a "reminder" somewhere else in the house.

Boxes are also available with plastic lips around the edge that fold in and help keep litter from spilling or being tossed out as the cat scratches. Again, make sure your cat will use this type of box and can easily get in and out of it.

Self-cleaning litter boxes have been on the market for several years now, yet I only know a small number of people who use them. These litter boxes work by sifting the litter mechanically and pushing it into a tray that can be removed and dumped easily. Some concerns have been that the cat would get hurt or startled as the mechanism moves to rake the litter. I have spoken with the owners of these litter boxes and they have revealed no problems. The boxes are created to stop very easily if anything touches the mechanism. Also, the machine "waits" about ten minutes after the cat has left the box before the rake is activated. Clumping litters are the only choice to use with these boxes, as the mechanism can only remove clumps of material. These boxes are not recommended for kittens.

As for the price, when they first came out these litter containment systems ran around $200. Many people just simply could not afford them. Now they cost under $100, and you can generally find one on an online auction (such as eBay, www.ebay.com) for much less.

Dry-system litter boxes come equipped with an aeration system and replaceable pads that absorb and dry urine before odors can develop. They must be used with a special type of rock litter that is periodically washed. These systems are available through some pet supply catalogs and retailers, and are expensive. However, you do save the cost of buying fresh litter all the time.

Regardless of the type of box you choose, make sure it is one your cat will be able and willing to use, and is not too big or too small for the cat you have.

## Where to Put the Box?

Most cats, like humans, prefer a little privacy in the toilet. The decision of where to place your cat's litter box should be based on this fact, as well as the space available in your home, accessibility for the cat, convenience, and your personal preference.

Putting the litter box in a basement or other room your cat rarely frequents will probably result in a mess elsewhere, particularly during times of stress or if the cat has a bowel upset due to illness or something he ate. If, however, your cat spends much of his time hunting for spiders (or whatever else he enjoys) in the basement, then placing the litter box there is not a bad idea.

If you have the room, and particularly if you have more than one cat, two or more litter boxes in different locations is a good idea. If you have three or more cats, you will definitely need more than one litter box. Having just one box for that many cats can be too trying on the nerves (yours and your cats').

It's important to remember that, regardless of where you choose to place the box, it should be in an area free from excessive noise and movement, and away from where the cat eats and sleeps. But it must be in a location the cat can get to easily and willingly. And make sure your cat knows where it is by bringing him to the box.

Your bathroom is the most frequent, and obvious, location for a litter box. Usually bathrooms are quiet and out of the way of heavy traffic (unless you are having a party—then kitty can be placed, litter box and all, in a room away from the noise), and if you use a flushable litter, cleaning the box is simplified.

There are many ways to hide a litter box creatively and still enable the cat to find it conveniently. The box can be placed under a sink (provided there is enough room, easy access for the cat, no harmful chemicals nearby, and your cat knows where to find the box). Most pet supply companies sell attractive screens specifically made to be placed around a litter box.

With a little imagination and carpentry skills, you can build a cabinet or shelter for the box. If you do, make sure to allow plenty of room for the cat and box and an easily accessible opening not only for the cat but also for you to remove the box. Also, it's a good idea to place a hole in the side where you can fasten a screen or provide some other way for the odor to escape. Otherwise the odors may permeate and ruin the cat box shelter, and many cats will refuse to use it if it smells.

Children love sandboxes to play in, and to some children, the cat box is the best—an indoor sandbox always available for their enjoyment. The best solution to this problem is to put the litter box where the child cannot get to it. This can be a cabinet or a separate room with the door kept closed to keep the child out. Of course, if you do this, you must find a way for the cat to get in the room, but not the child. Many stores and catalogs sell cat doors, or you can build one yourself.

I have seen many imaginative and interesting things done with cat boxes to hide them from human view. You can easily try any number of things, keeping in mind the ease of cleaning and the accessibility to the cat. Or you can do what I do: simply place open cat boxes in various locations, making no attempt to hide them at all—and keeping them extra clean.

## Litter Box Liners

Litter box liners can be used to keep litter and odors from sticking to the box and to help with cleaning. Rather than dumping the litter when it becomes soiled, a litter liner enables you to simply lift the entire "package" right out of the box.

Cats rarely scratch only the litter, however. They also get the side and bottom of the box, the wall behind the box and even the floor. Cats with all claws intact usually tear liners when they scratch, spilling litter back into the box and defeating the purpose of the liner.

Most people choose to line their boxes with newspaper, which can aid in cleaning and prevent litter from sticking to the bottom of the box. But, as with liners, cats will eventually rip newspapers to shreds.

## Maintenance and Odor Control

On the whole, I think if cats could philosophize, the most popular philosophy they would come up with is that a litter box can never be too clean. That means no matter how much you may hate it, there's no getting around the daily scooping and regular scrubbing.

When placing litter in the box, try not to put in too much or too little. Too much litter is harder to clean as the urine seeps to the bottom (and will also add to the spillage), and too little will not absorb properly and will need to be cleaned constantly. One to two inches of litter is generally recommended, but I have found that it depends on the litter box, the cat, and how many cats are using the box(es). How many times you need to scoop per day should determine the depth of the litter. If you have only one cat, one scoop per day should be enough. More than one cat, however, warrants two scoops per day, or even three in large multicat households. And the more scooping, the more litter you'll need to make up for what you take out.

Odors are caused by bacteria, and bacteria are everywhere. Just scooping the litter box is not enough to keep these microscopic creatures away from your cat and out of your home. The box must be emptied completely and the litter changed every few days with traditional, nonclumping litters and at least once a month with clumping litters. The box should also be washed every time you change the litter, using an antibacterial detergent that is safe for pets. Pet supply stores carry many brands of cleaning agents that neutralize odors and will not make your cat ill with harmful odors or ingredients.

You can use a diluted bleach solution to clean the box more thoroughly once every month or two, if you feel the odors are building up within the box (remember that plastic is porous and tends to hold smells). But be

*The right litter scoop is an important part of your cleaning process.*

careful: bleach is harmful to cats if they breathe it in or lick it from the box or their paws. Make sure the bleach is thoroughly rinsed from the box before refilling it with litter (a good test is that if you can smell the bleach, so can your cat).

After many years of keeping saltwater fish and, on occasion, bleaching coral, I have learned that a good way to get rid of bleach odors is to place the item in the sun, allowing the heat to bake the bleach out.

You can do this with litter boxes, too. After rinsing as thoroughly as possible, place the empty litter box in the sunshine for the day. When you can no longer smell even the slightest trace of bleach, rinse the box again (you can never be too safe), dry it, and refill it. When you do this, it's good idea to have a backup litter box to use while the other one is sunning.

Keeping the litter dry is another way to prevent odors and bacteria from multiplying. And after washing the box out, dry it thoroughly before refilling it with litter. You don't want to trap moisture beneath the litter before the cat even uses it. Scooping two or three times a day will keep the litter sifted, helping it to stay dry. Make sure, however, that when you scoop, you get to the bottom of the box.

Cats don't always hit the right area on the litter box when they go. Accidents can drip down the side and make quite a mess. Instead of emptying out the whole box and washing it when this happens, wipe the area well using deodorizing antibacterial wipes (usually they come in oval containers and as you pull them through the small hole in the top, they separate at the perforation). After you have wiped the area down, dry it thoroughly with a paper towel. These deodorizing wipes are good for many cat cleaning duties, as long as you are careful to dry the area thoroughly before your cat walks on it.

Sometimes, regardless of what you do or how well you clean the box, after awhile it simply gets too dirty to be cleaned. Plastic is porous, and eventually bacteria seeps in and ruins the box. If you can, replace the litter box every year or two, helping to keep your cat's area fresh.

A good habit to get into, and one that I follow daily, is to keep an eye on the contents of the litter box as you scoop. This way, if there is any problem, such as bloody urine or diarrhea, you will spot it before it gets out of hand and can take steps to find out which cat is ill or get a stool sample to the veterinarian.

Even if you keep your cat's box exceptionally clean, there may still be the occasional accident. A cat who has a bowel or bladder problem may not be able to hold it long enough to get to the box, or may drip as he runs. To clean up these accidents and control their odors, it is best to get to them as soon as they are made. This is not always possible, but the sooner you get to the mess (especially with urine), the better your chance will be of cleaning it efficiently. If urine is allowed to soak into any surface (particularly carpets), there is a greater chance the cat will reuse that area as his toilet, or another cat may use the same spot. Use an enzymatic cleaner and let it soak into the carpet. The enzymes will break down the urine, removing the "food" that bacteria feed on. Odor neutralizers are also available that can be used to clean the area, and sprays can kill odors in a specific spot.

The idea is to get rid of the smell, not cover it up. Cats have very sensitive olfactory nerves and can smell the urine even beneath some of the strongest-smelling products. For that reason, avoid cleaning up accidents with ammonia, because its lingering scent smells a lot like cat urine.

## Toilet Training

A cat on a toilet? Believe it or not, some people have successfully toilet-trained their cats. Pet supply shops and some gift catalogs sell cat toilet-training kits that come with a specially designed seat cover,

*Some cats can be trained to use the toilet. But you'll have to leave the lid up for them.*

instructions, and herbs that are attractive to cats. The idea is to place the special seat cover over your toilet seat, so it becomes a sort of makeshift litter box. Litter is placed inside, and is slowly removed as the cat learns that this is where he is to do his business. Eventually the special seat cover is removed, and the cat eliminates into the toilet—very convenient for the owner. Teaching your cat to flush, however, is up to you.

The sight of a cat squatting over the toilet is quite a humorous one. This method is more successful for the owner of one or two cats, rather than for a house full of cats. Not every cat will do it. And not every cat owner wants the cat using their toilet seat.

## Litter Box Problems

Sylvester, a neutered male, is good about using the litter box—except when a new cat comes into the house. Suddenly he begins eliminating on the carpets and occasionally on clothing left in baskets. This behavior usually lasts a few months, until the new cat is comfortably integrated into the hierarchy of the household and takes on the familiar scent of the house.

Territorial marking, as Sylvester exhibits, is only one of the many reasons a cat may suddenly stop using the litter box. Refusal to use the box is the number-one behavioral problem in cats and one of the biggest reasons cats are turned in to shelters. At some point in their lives, 10 percent of all cats develop a problem associated with the litter box.

Finding the reason a cat is not using his litter box, or why he has suddenly stopped using it, can be a challenge. The very first step to take is a trip to the veterinarian. Often cats with a physical problem, such as a urinary tract disorder (FLUTD; see chapter 8), will begin to associate the discomfort they feel from the illness with the litter box, because of the pain that's present whenever they climb into the box to relieve themselves. This sudden negative association with their litter box can make them decide the box is the cause of their troubles, and is best avoided.

If a visit to the vet rules out any physical problem, you will have to do a little detective work. If your cat has suddenly decided he would rather relieve himself on your Persian carpet than in his box, think about why and try to eliminate the problem. Here are a few of the more common reasons a cat may stop using his box.

## The Box Itself

This can include the size of the box, the style of box, or even the material the box is made of. Some cats have problems with covered boxes or the odd shape of self-cleaning boxes, so if you have recently purchased one and your cat refuses to use it, you have basically two choices:

1.  Get rid of the box and go back to using the tried-and-true version you had before.

2.  Try to retrain the cat to use the box. This involves showing the cat that there is nothing to fear from this new device by gently bringing him to the box and showing it to him. Speak in a soothing tone of voice and do not hold the cat there if he wishes to run away. If you show the cat often enough that this box is not going to harm him, he may soon be using it the way he did the old box.

Cats may also be picky about the material the box is made of. Commercial litter boxes are almost always made from a hard, durable plastic that is accepted by cats. But I have seen some people who make litter boxes out of other items, such as metal pans, boxes (wood or cardboard), and other materials that may or may not be acceptable to the cat or easily cleaned by the owner. If the litter box is made of a material that seems strange to the cat (either because of its smell or its feel beneath his paws), he may reject it. In any case, a litter box should be made of a material that is easy to clean because, as mentioned above, cats often will not use a box that they consider dirty or smelly.

## Type of Litter

Certain deodorizing litters or sprinkle-on deodorizers can irritate some cats' nasal passages and even their feet. This may cause them to avoid the litter box altogether and use an area more familiar, such as your carpet. Try a plain, low-dust cat litter with no scent or deodorizers.

If you're thinking of switching litters, remember that cats don't usually enjoy changes to their environment. I have found that occasionally switching litters will cause some of my cats to avoid the box. To remedy this problem, I gradually add more and more of the new litter to the old litter over a period of days or even weeks, enabling the cats to slowly adjust to the new litter. You may have to stick with your old litter if your cat simply will not accept a change.

## New Cat, New Location

A new cat in the house may not know right away where the litter box is. That's why it is imperative to show the cat where the litter box is several times a day for the first few days (see chapter 2 for more on introducing a new cat into your home).

Changing the location of the litter box can also cause confusion. If the litter box is normally kept in the bathroom and later it is moved to the hallway, often the cat will continue to use the area where the litter box once was. In a case like this, it will be necessary not only to show the cat where the litter box is now kept, but also to make the place where the box used to be unattractive or inaccessible to the cat (the section "Training and Retraining" later in this chapter will explain how).

## Declawing

Surgery to remove a cat's claws is a process that leaves the paws sensitive, making litter seem too rough and painful. Often, when a cat returns from this surgery he will refuse to use the litter box. Using a softer litter may help, but occasionally the cat will continue to fear the box even after his paws have healed.

Sometimes moving the location of the litter box or adding a new litter box will help. If not, retraining the cat to use his box and to reassociate the box with something positive will be required (see "Training and Retraining" later in this chapter). Shredded newspapers or litters made from recycled newspaper should be used for two weeks after declaw surgery, as they are easier on sensitive feet.

## Territorial Disputes

This mostly takes the form of urine spraying, which can be done either in the usual squatting position or by backing up to a vertical surface such as the wall. Marking is an instinctual behavior. In the wild, cats mark out an area that they consider theirs. This is communication; the cat is leaving an odoriferous message that tells other cats to stay away from that area.

Cats also mark when they feel their territory is threatened or invaded by another cat. Just because a cat is kept indoors does not always mean this instinctual behavior will be eliminated. With a cat who feels a strong urge to mark, simply marking in the litter box is not enough.

New people, odors, and other cats or animals can make a territorial cat feel he needs to redefine his own particular location. A cat may even spray an object or piece of clothing that smells unfamiliar or smells of another cat. The cat may not even know why he is marking, but just feels that he must.

If there are other cats roaming around near your home, your cat may also feel the urge to mark. Even though those cats are outside and your cat is inside, he may feel the outsiders are on his turf and he needs to send them an olfactory message. Often the cat will mark near windows or doors.

A cat who has reached sexual maturity (about 6 months old) and has not yet been altered, a cat who is in heat, or a male cat who senses a female cat nearby may spray to signal availability or to show other cats "this is my turf." Usually having a male cat neutered before any of this behavior begins, or a female spayed before her first heat, can prevent this type of spraying entirely. But on occasion even some altered cats may spray. Usually, once the perceived threat has passed the behavior will pass, too.

## Fear

A fearful cat may suddenly stop using his litter box. If something happened near the box to frighten the cat, he will see the box as the source of his fear and will not want to go near it.

A shy cat or a cat bullied by another cat may feel on guard at all times and will not want to venture too far to reach a crowded litter box. A cat like this should have his own litter box placed near the area where he spends most of his time.

## Stress

In chapter 3 I discussed the many reasons indoor cats may become stressed, and I don't need to repeat that information here. But it is important to remember that stress is one of the most major factors involved in litter box lapses.

Sometimes taking a trip will cause a kind of separation anxiety in cats that manifests itself in indiscriminate urination. My stepfather, a retired truck driver, was often gone for two or three days at a time. His late cat Sylvia would, on occasion, leave him a "reminder" in his overnight bag that she was there and did not want him to leave her. It's a strange way of showing affection, but that is, in a sense, one way a feline says, "I love you, don't leave me."

## Jealousy

This goes hand in hand with stress. A new baby in the house who takes up the attention you used to give the cat is a common cause of jealously. A new marriage or a new pet can also prompt a cat to show his disapproval by eliminating inappropriately. In any new situation in your cat's life, make sure you prepare the cat in advance by introducing him slowly to whatever change is to come. For instance, show the cat the baby's things and items associated with a baby before the

actual arrival of the infant. Or have your fiancé visit often and interact with the cats. Let him or her leave an item of clothing in your
house so the cat will become familiar with the scent.

## Stray and Feral Cats

Cats who were born, raised, or lived a long time outdoors may not
know what a litter box is, particularly if they were trained from the
start that the ground is their litter box. In this case, slow but thorough
retraining will be essential. A fine-grain, sandlike litter should be
used, or you can start out with dirt and work up to litter slowly. With
these cats, a clean litter box is extremely important.

## Competition

How many cats occupy your house and use the litter boxes? Certain
cats will be picky about using a litter box frequented by other cats.
You should provide enough litter boxes for the number of cats in the
household, based on how well the cats get along. In my house, some
of the cats are not part of the small social hierarchy and are reluctant
to use the litter boxes frequented by the cats who are. To remedy this
problem, a couple of the cats have separate litter boxes that are, for
the most part, used only by them.

Some experts recommend having one litter box per cat. This is fine
if you have only two or three cats and want each cat to have his own
box. But what if you have seven, or even twelve or more cats? You
certainly do not want every inch of floor space taken up by litter
boxes! I believe one box for every two cats is sufficient, unless a cat
needs to have his own box.

## Dirty Box

We all know how fastidiously clean cats are. Their sniffers are much
more sensitive than ours. Every cat is different when it comes to litter
box cleanliness. Some will tolerate a fair bit of mess, but I know of
several cats who will not go in a litter box that is even slightly soiled.
Instead, they will go on the floor beside the box. See the section

"Maintenance and Odor Control" earlier in this chapter for more on keeping the box clean.

### Location

The location of the litter box is important. Some cats relish privacy and may choose a remote spot as their bathroom if the litter box is in a high-traffic area. Also, some cats grow accustomed to the particular location of the box. If the box is moved, the cat may continue to go where the box once was. If it's necessary to move the box, try moving it just a short distance at a time until it's in its new location, or distract or restrict the cat from where the box used to be until he is completely used to the new place.

### Box Size

Who says size doesn't matter? Not cats, when it comes to their litter box. If the box is too small, your cat may feel cramped and uncomfortable inside and need more room. If the box is too large, especially for a young kitten or an older cat, he may have trouble getting in and out.

### Liners

Some cats simply reject the idea of liners in their boxes. A shy cat may be frightened by the crinkling sound of the liner as he scratches. Newspaper may have similar negative effects.

## Training and Retraining

Kittens learn litter box etiquette from their mothers, who teach them where to go, and to bury and cover their waste. The rest is instinct. Even cats who were not trained to use the litter box early on by their mother have shown signs of knowing instinctively how to rake their paws through dirt.

A mother cat usually begins teaching her kittens about the litter box between 3 and 4 weeks of age. Generally, when you acquire a kitten, he will be at least 6 to 8 weeks of age or older, so this will already be accomplished, and all you will need to do is remind your new pet where the litter box is the first few days. However, if a younger kitten has fallen into your hands, or if you acquire a kitten who does not seem to know what the litter box is used for, you will have to step in as a surrogate mother (or father).

Remember, your best chance for success will be to first set up everything to the kitty's liking: proper location, size and type of box, comfortable litter, and most of all patience and perseverance.

Kitty will need to be shown the litter box regularly and at times when a kitten (or cat) would normally do his business. The most common times are after naps, playtime, and meals, just like a human baby. Set the kitten in the box, speak in a soothing tone, and carefully and gently move his front paws in a digging motion once or twice. If the kitten begins to sniff around, back away and give him some privacy. Don't force the kitten to stay in the box if he doesn't wish to. You want to use positive reinforcement rather than force, which will give the box a negative association. Don't even use something like a squirt gun if the kitten or cat has an accident. All this will do is tell the cat he is doing something wrong by taking care of his natural urges and will only confuse him.

After you've shown your cat the box a few times, he should get the hang of what is supposed to be done there. Continue to show the kitten the box, taking him there regularly and watching for telltale signs that he has the urge to go (sniffing around, scratching), until the kitten is using the box on his own.

Retraining a cat or kitten who has always used the box but has now stopped for some reason may take more time. Success will depend on eliminating whatever caused the behavior to begin with; retraining will only work if you also remedy the cause of the cat's trouble. Never yell at or scold the cat, because this may only make matters worse.

As with training a kitten, retraining should be done with patience, using positive reinforcement.

You may need to move the location of the litter box for retraining, particularly if the problem was one associated with fear. The location alone may frighten the cat, and putting the box (or better yet, a new box) in a different place may eliminate the problem. A cat who is being bullied may need a litter box placed in close proximity to where he spends most of his time (preferably his own box, not to be used by any other cat).

If surgery or an illness was the cause of the cat's refusal to use the box, try a new litter. The different experience may help to break the cat's old association of the litter box with a painful problem. In a case like this, moving or changing the box can also be helpful.

Try placing several boxes in different locations, even if you have only one cat. If you find the cat likes to urinate in the box but defecate elsewhere (or vice versa), try two boxes. One box should be kept in its usual location. The other box you can place where the cat seems to be eliminating most frequently, gradually moving the box until it is where you want it to be. Or you can try placing a small amount of the cat's stool in the new box in the location where you want it. (Only a small amount, though. Remember, cats like cleanliness.) Show the cat the box frequently, speaking soothingly and maybe moving his paws to show him he has a new place to choose. Retrain your cat with frequent trips to the litter box, in much the same way as training a kitten was described earlier.

### Online Resources

For more on helping your cat learn or relearn litter box etiquette, please try the following Web sites:

www.perfectpaws.com/litter.html
www.valleyhumanesociety.org/know/catbehavior
www.catsinternational.org
www.phsspca.org/training/litterbox.htm

When you're not home to supervise, try confining the cat to a room with his litter box, food, and water. A small room is best (I made a small room for one of my cats in an area beneath the stairs) so that the cat will be less likely to use the floor and more likely to use the box. Confinement does not have to be permanent. Once the cat is using the box regularly, you can try letting him out of confinement and see how things go.

Try your best to limit the cat's access to the spot where he has been eliminating inappropriately. Close the door to that room, if possible. If not, cover the area with something the cat does not like to walk on, such as aluminum foil, bubble wrap, double-sided tape, or a plastic tarp or shower curtain. Placing your cat's food and water dishes on the spot where he has his accidents (especially if he seems to like one particular location) may also help prevent the cat from going back to that area. Cats do not like to eat where they eliminate. Clean the area well with an enzymatic cleaner before placing the food and water dishes there.

Sometimes you may have to experiment with different methods before finding one that works with your cat. Just remember, however, that cats like to feel comfortable. By simulating as best you can the area a cat would use if he were outside, you have a greater chance of success.

## Diapers

As a last resort, if your cat simply refuses to use the litter box or if you are in the process of retraining, you might want to try diapers. Yes, diapers. It sounds strange and looks stranger, but if your cat will wear them, it is preferable to putting the cat down or giving him up.

Cat breeders sometimes use them for their intact males, who will often spray quite a bit in a cattery. I don't mean Huggies or a pinned-on cloth; the diapers best used for a cat are actually heat harnesses/pads for dogs. For most cats, the petite or extra-small sizes work the best.

Some of these are simply material that is fastened around the animal's back end, around the tail. Others are pretty and elaborate—underwear for your pet. Whichever style you choose, you will want something more absorbent than the pads offered for dogs in heat. Maxi pads designed for women work best for absorbing abundant liquid such as urine.

If you have an outdoor cat you are converting to an indoor pet, simulating his outdoor environment is a must. Find a litter that best imitates the surface area the cat likes the most. If you keep the litter box in an out-of-the-way area and your cat insists on going in the kitchen, try moving the box to the kitchen (or placing one box in each location).

No one but the cat knows all his reasons for everything he does. Sometimes a cat will suddenly decide, for no apparent reason, that he no longer likes his box or the litter. He will either stop using it altogether or stop one litter box activity and not the other (for example, urinating in the box but defecating on the carpet). To the cat there is a reason for this. But to you that reason may seem unfathomable.

In severe cases where every possible means has been tried, every possible solution gone over, you may want to talk to your vet about medication for the cat (a temporary solution that may or may not help) or about recommending a feline behavior therapist. Perhaps together you can come up with the answer.

# 5

# The Claws That Scratch

The large black-and-white tuxedo cat stared, perplexed, at the small scratching post her caretakers had recently bought. She knew her old, and favorite, scratching area had been removed and replaced by one that did not smell like home, but nevertheless, it had to be marked as part of her territory. So the claws came out and tore through the new fabric, feeling wonderful between her paws, stretching her muscles, and giving her confidence.

Her caretakers seemed most displeased, though she did not understand why. Where else was she supposed to stretch and shed the outer sheaths of her claws, as all cats must? On this small, unstable carpeted post they threw in front of her? It would not possibly suit for those activities!

First of all, the post was far too short, and she could not reach up and get a really good stretch. And when she tried to pull her claws through the raggedy carpet on the post, it began to tip toward her. Instinct told her this would not be safe. If she were to give this small carpeted statue a good yank with her strong claws, it would be pulled down on top of her. So what was she to do? The sofa was so much better!

## Why Cats Scratch

It grates on the nerves like the sound of fingernails across a blackboard—that horrible ripping and tearing of cat claws in your sofa. But don't despair. There is hope, and you don't have to send your cat packing if she decides to use your sofa for a scratching post.

As with anything regarding cats, it's important to understand the reason behind your cat's behavior so you can determine the best way to redirect it.

Your cat does not scratch the sofa, carpet, or drapes (or any other inappropriate object) out of malice or spite. She is simply acting out an instinctual behavior. Cats need to scratch, and there are three good reasons why.

First, scratching removes the outer sheath of the claw, shedding it something like a snake sheds its skin. This sharpens the claws: as the hull is stripped away, a new, sharper claw is left behind. This keeps the cat's defense capabilities at maximum and provides the cat with a swift escape from predators. Fortunately for the indoor cat, her most formidable predator is the vacuum cleaner, but the physical structure of the claw remains the same even if the cat does not go outside.

 **Online Resources**

For more on cat scratching behavior, see:

www.maxshouse.com/ understanding_ scratching.htm

Second, like urine spraying, scratching is also a form of territory marking. The bottoms of a cat's feet are filled not only with tiny capillaries that dilate and perspire (which helps the cat regulate her body temperature), but also with scent glands. When a cat scratches, she leaves a physical mark that other cats can see, and also a scent marker that clearly states this is her area. Often a cat will touch you with her paws, letting you know that you are her human.

Third, cats scratch to stretch the muscles in their paws, back, and legs. Just as humans stretch when they awaken or after sitting for a long time, so do cats. They use their claws to anchor their front half so they can get a good stretch throughout the rest of their body. This is good for the cat's health.

Those are the three most common reasons cats use their claws, but they are used for many other purposes, as well. When your cat was a kitten and still nursing from her mother, she used her tiny paws and little needlelike claws to knead at the teats, which helped stimulate milk flow. As adults, most cats still indulge in kneading behavior when they are content, a throwback to the behavior that gave them such positive results in kittenhood. Unfortunately for us, however, most cats still use their now talonlike claws when kneading, often on your lap.

My cat Sammy loves my long hair. At night, he sometimes curls himself up in it as if it were another cat and kneads at the back of my head. Keeping his nails trimmed can help make this loving behavior more pleasant.

Cats also use their claws to scratch themselves. There's nothing like a good scratch when something itches, and cat claws are perfect for this. Although cats generally use only the hind paws for scratching itches, they use their front paws for grooming, and this sometimes includes the claws.

## The Mechanics of Claws

Other than cheetahs, all types of cats have retractable claws. This means that the cat can sheath her claws and extend them at will.

(Kittens, however, are not able to retract their claws until they are about 4 weeks of age.) Most cats have eighteen claws all around: four on each back paw and four, plus a dewclaw (up on the leg, above the foot), on each front paw.

A cat's claws are an extension of her skin, a complex part of

*A cat's claws are made to retract.*

the epidermal structure, and are attached to the last bone of the toes. The nerves and blood vessels that run through the claw form the

## Something Extra

*Candy is a polydactyl cat.*

Polydactyl, a word that sounds more like a dinosaur than a cat, is the term used for cats who have extra "fingers" (often called "double-pawed"). Many polydactyl cats have extended dewclaws that resemble a thumb, but the gene that produces polydactylism is often responsible for the cat having more than the usual number of claws, as well.

pinkish line you can see running into the claw. This is called the quick.

The dead, white outer layer of tissue must be sloughed off regularly to expose the new growth underneath. If it is not removed, the nail continues to grow and can cause health problems. It interferes with mobility because the cat's claws get caught as she walks, and if allowed to grow too far the claw can actually grow back into the pads of the paws. It's important to allow your cat to scratch as she needs to. Keeping the claws clipped also helps keep the nails in shape.

# Cat Trees and Posts

I have known too many people who gave up their indoor cats or began allowing them outside because the cat was scratching their furniture, carpets, walls, and other surfaces, and the owner was tired of the expense of replacing the items. In each of these cases, I asked the owners if they had a scratching post or cat tree in their house. The answer was always no.

You can't assume a cat will simply give up an instinctive behavior just because her owner has not made the appropriate resource available. The cat will find her own resources—in other words, she will scratch whatever is available and seems appropriate.

You know your cat needs to scratch. The trick now is to make sure your cat knows where to scratch and where not to. In other words, you must redirect your cat's natural instincts from the inappropriate area to an appropriate one. To do this, you must first provide the cat with something that suits you both.

Cat trees and posts come in almost as many shapes, sizes, and colors as cats do. Finding a scratching post or tree to fit your home shouldn't be difficult. The key is finding ones that suit your cat's scratching tastes. Every cat is different and each has her own preference for scratching surfaces. Buying a cat tree or post your cat refuses to use (for whatever reason) is a useless exercise. You might as well not have one at all.

In our house we have several cat trees. In the living room a very tall multitiered post stands in front of a window. Two of the posts leading up to the tiers are natural wood and the third is wrapped in sisal rope. The tiers, tube, and base are carpeted. This type of tree is one of the best, because it gives the cat variety in her choice of textures and surfaces. A few of our cats prefer to scratch natural wood— one cat in particular always used the wood trim on the walls until we replaced it with plastic trim and bought the scratching tree.

There is another cat tree in the house as well. That one is smaller but sturdy, and is made of carpet and sisal rope. It has large rectangular "beds" on each tier and the cats love sleeping in them. Even the largest cat fits well inside these high cat beds, and the sides offer a nice feeling of security.

When we first brought the large tree into our living room, the cats went bonkers. They ran up it at breakneck speed, scratched every post and perch, attacked one another playfully, and chased each other up and down. With a cat on each perch, they would bat at each other from above and below. Of course, that initial enthusiasm has worn off somewhat, but the fact of the matter is that they have not touched the sofa since. And the tree is still used daily for play and sleep, as well as scratching and stretching.

*There is no substitute for a cat tree your cat can do more with than simply scratch.*

When you're shopping for a cat tree or post for your cat, keep in mind your cat's particular desires, preferences, and personality. Ask yourself several questions: Where does your cat like to scratch and what surfaces seem to be her favorites? Where does your cat spend most of her time and in what room does she do the most scratching?

In addition to these questions, base your buying decision on common sense and the innate behavior of all cats. As men-tioned earlier, cats scratch for

*Cats enjoy the roominess and sense of security offered by these tiers.*

several reasons, and these reasons should be kept in mind when you're shopping for a tree or post for your cat(s) to scratch.

First, cats scratch to slough their claws, and for this they like a scratching surface they can really dig their claws into. Therefore, you need to buy a tree with a surface your cat prefers. Some cats like to scratch the carpet. Carpeted posts are the most common and come in a variety of colors that can match your furniture. Some cats like the rough surface of the back of carpeting. I remember one time I bought carpeting for the house. I placed the roll in the kitchen leaning up against the dishwasher. The cats were all over it, scratching and using it as a makeshift bridge to climb up. I've never seen a tree or post made with the back side of the carpet facing out, but you can easily attach a carpet remnant, back side out, right over an old post. Sisal rope trees and posts, with their rough surface almost like that of the back side of carpet, can sometimes be an acceptable alternative. Tightly woven fabrics, hemp, bark, and even corrugated cardboard are all good surfaces that a cat can dig into and not only remove the hulls from her claws, but also get in a good stretch.

Scratching is also a form of territory marking, your cat's way of saying, "This area is mine." This innate behavior is an important one to consider when deciding where you will put the tree or post. Where your cat prefers to do her scratching should be where you place her scratching furniture. Most cats seem to prefer the living room furniture, but I have also known cats who like the walls, and even the kitchen table. If you place the tree or post in one room when the cat does most of her scratching in another room, you've just wasted your money. She may use the post or tree on occasion, but she will also continue to use your sofa, or whatever other surface she prefers, in the room she prefers to be in.

Cats love to look out the window. A tree with tiers for the cat to rest on, placed in front of a window, will ensure its use. A window with a view of bird feeders will raise the chances of the tree being in almost constant use.

Last, and definitely not least, is the fact that cats stretch when they scratch. A cat will not use a tree or post that is going to tip over or move whenever she digs her claws into it and pulls. Buy a tree or post with a good, solid base. The base should be larger in diameter than the top or the largest part of the main area of the tree or post. I test the tree myself while it's still in the store. I tug at the top as if I were a cat climbing up it. If it tips easily, I move on to the next one.

It is also important to take into account the cat's size when fully stretched out. A post that is too short won't do the cat much good, since cats like to stretch to their full length when scratching. The average scratching post is usually too short for this; look for one that is more than three feet high.

Although most cat trees are more expensive than a simple post, they are also more widely preferred by cats, for obvious reasons. If you are worried about expense, weigh the price of one really good cat tree against the price of periodically replacing your sofa, and you will see that the benefits outweigh the cost. In the long run, you will save money and you and your cat will be happier.

In addition to cat trees and posts that are set on a base, there are also many types of scratching pads and hang-off-the-door scratching furniture available commercially. Some are impregnated with catnip to draw the cat to them. Most are made of corrugated cardboard (which some cats will scratch, others will ignore), and there are even carpeted pads available that you can attach to the wall. Some

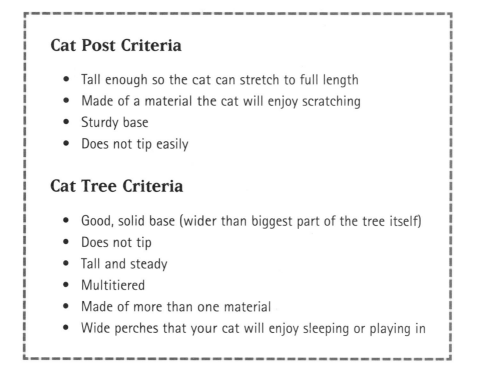

## Cat Post Criteria

- Tall enough so the cat can stretch to full length
- Made of a material the cat will enjoy scratching
- Sturdy base
- Does not tip easily

## Cat Tree Criteria

- Good, solid base (wider than biggest part of the tree itself)
- Does not tip
- Tall and steady
- Multitiered
- Made of more than one material
- Wide perches that your cat will enjoy sleeping or playing in

cats may be just fine with these, but often they are not enough. Either they are not stable enough and tend to tip or move, or they are not large enough for the cat to use to full advantage. If your cat will use these, great. But if they are all that's provided, often a cat will use them along with your sofa. Usually it's better, for you and the cat, to buy a good-quality scratching tree or post that meets all the cat's needs.

For all the reasons mentioned, scratching trees that are made of two or three different materials are best. Usually you can find posts that are made all of carpet; trees made from carpet, wood and rope; and a variety of other combinations. The more choices you give your cat, the better the chance that she will prefer her post or tree to your furniture. With one cat, the tree you buy may not have to be as elaborate as the one you will need if you have many cats, but the tree should still be tall, sturdy, and effective.

*A large enough cat tree can be shared with a buddy.*

I cannot stress enough the importance of a good, sturdy, tall cat tree! Chances are you can find one that is less expensive than declawing surgery would cost, and your cat will definitely prefer the tree. Simply put, if your sofa, chairs, and other furniture are more fun to climb, scratch, and run up and down than the tree or post you provide, your cat will use your sofa, chairs, and other furniture! Buy a tree your cat can have fun on.

## One Post or Two?

Someone once asked me why her cat was still using the sofa and other furniture to satisfy his urge to scratch, even though she had provided him with a scratching post. The first question I asked her was what type of post she provided for him. "Just a regular post," was her answer. "How tall is it? What is it made of? Is it the only post in the house?" After several questions, I discovered this post was not only too small for her cat, but it was the only area in the entire house she provided that was suitable for scratching. I recommended she spend the money to buy a tall tree made from different materials and place that in the cat's favorite area, and then put the scratching post in another area of the house that the cat uses.

Too often, people think all they have to do is buy one cheap little post and their cat will automatically use it and leave everything else in the house alone. But generally the post ends up untouched and the furniture continues to be destroyed.

Experts recommend, for good reason, that you provide more than one scratching area for your cat. Often cats will scratch in more than one place, and if you place a scratching pad, post, or tree in each location where she likes to scratch, you will lower the odds of your cat using your furniture.

In a multicat household, more than one scratching area is a necessity. Trees with multiple tiers provide places to scratch, plus places to sleep and play. As with any area of the house, a group of cats will establish territories. More than one scratching tree provides the cats with a variety of places to sleep and play, thereby lessening the chance that a fight will break out. Also, it will provide the cats with plenty of places to mark their territory.

You can buy different types of trees, posts, and pads to place in various locations, but it's important to place them in areas that your cat(s) scratch. For one cat, a smaller but good-quality tree plus a smaller, stable post is usually sufficient (though, as with anything, there are exceptions). If your cat will use the cardboard pads and still likes to scratch many areas around the house, try placing a good-quality tree or post in her favorite spot, and the cardboard or smaller pads everywhere else. The more cats you have, the more posts and trees should be provided.

"But I've just obtained a new cat and don't know where or what she likes to scratch yet," you might say. In a case like this, your best bet is to buy one or two trees or posts made with a variety of materials and place them in the most obvious locations—wherever there are surfaces a cat would like to scratch, such as the living room with its perfectly scratchable furniture. It helps to buy several posts and trees and place them in various locations before the cat arrives. Then you can always move them if you find your new cat scratching an area where there is no tree or post.

## Scratching Post Training

Here comes the tricky part. You bought your trees and posts and have placed them strategically around the house. Now you must get your cat to use them! I hardly had to train my cats at all once we bought the multitiered tree. It was so much more fun than the furniture that the cats preferred it. But there are still occasions when a cat will have to be chased away from the chair.

Placing the post or tree in an area your cat frequents is a start, but sometimes cats will scratch the tree and post as well as the furniture. You have to make sure your cat knows where it's appropriate to use her claws and where it is not allowed.

As I mentioned in chapter 2 about teaching a new cat the house rules, make sure when you bring a cat into the house that you show her from the start where her own furniture is. If you catch her scratching an inappropriate area, use a squirt bottle (remember, no hitting) to chase the cat away from that area.

Or you can simply pick her up and immediately place the cat by the tree. Show her that this is the right place by scratching the post with your own nails and then taking the cat's paws and moving them up and down the post, much the way you train a kitten to use the litter box (see chapter 4). Say "Good kitty," and praise the cat, even if she doesn't scratch or just looks at you as if you are nuts. If the cat uses the post, it's time for a celebration. Let your cat know she just did something great.

Play with your cat near her post or on her tree. Some cat trees or posts come with toys built into them—yarn and balls or springs with pom-poms on them that most cats love to bat at. Playing with your cat will give her a positive association with her tree or post and help draw her there even when you are not available to play.

Catnip rubbed on the post or a catnip spray can also help attract the cat. But keep in mind that the effects of catnip only last for a short time and the catnip will eventually wear off. For this reason, it should be applied repeatedly during the cat's entire training, and even afterward as a reminder.

When you are not home to supervise, you may want to confine your cat to one room equipped with food, water, litter box, and scratching post. This way, you can be there to supervise when the cat has free run and does something wrong, or right. With a kitten, you can try the crate training explained in chapter 2.

But confinement shouldn't be necessary except in severe cases. Most cats will find that a really good cat tree made of carpet, wood, and rope is more fun and appealing than the furniture—particularly the tall, multitiered cat trees. I highly recommend those, simply because cats love them and can do so much more than just scratch them—more than they can do on a sofa.

## Breaking Bad Habits

So you have a cat who is already accustomed to your sofa or other furniture as her scratching place. Now what? This is a little more complicated to solve, but not impossible. At the same time you are attracting your cat to the right place to scratch, you should be doing what you can to make inappropriate places unattractive.

Pet supply stores and catalogs often sell plastic covers that can be fitted over the sides of your sofa to protect the material. There are also stick-on sofa protectors and double-sided tape strips that adhere to the sides of the sofa rather than fastening with pins.

Any type of surface that a cat does not like to scratch can work. Sometimes placing bubble wrap or aluminum foil over the area the cat likes to scratch can deter her from that area. Just about any smooth surface that does not allow the cat to get a grip with her claws can be used to cover your cat's favorite (but inappropriate) scratching spot.

With a little ingenuity, you can set up safe "traps," an object that makes noise when the cat scratches, or something small that falls and frightens the cat away from that area. I've even heard of people who have fastened balloons to the sofa so that the sound of them popping frightens the cat away.

**Online Resources**

If you wish to search for a good cat tree online, or products to help deter your cat from scratching, try the following:

www.createacatcondo.com

www.drsfostersmith.com

www.petsmart.com

www.petco.com/

www.angelicalcat.com/

Want to build your own cat tree? Look at amby.com/cat_site/cattree.html.

Of course, doing all this alone will not be enough, because soon your entire house will be covered from floor to ceiling with balloons, plastic, and aluminum foil. Not a pretty picture! You will also have to set out several cat trees in various locations, and use a firm but gentle hand to train. You can also find cat repellent sprays (make sure to get the ones for indoor use) that you can spray on your furniture to help keep your cat from scratching.

The type of furniture you have will also make a difference. Some materials are more scratchable than others. How about a sofa with a metal or a plastic wicker-look frame? No fun to scratch, so the cats leave these materials alone. Covering your sofa can also help quite a bit. My sofa is kept covered with a slipcover, and the cats have never scratched the sofa, not once. Sofa covers also keep the sofa clean, since they can be washed in the washing machine. Surefit (www .surefit.com) makes beautiful sofa covers that are designed to fit almost any size or shape sofa, and they come in many attractive colors and designs. These covers are fantastic for those whose sofas have already been ruined, because it will give the furniture a brand-new look. You can also get matching chair covers or have several different designs and change the look of your living area on a whim. Your cat will be able to sleep on the sofa, you will have an easy way to keep it clean, and most cats will not scratch furniture that is covered in this manner. These and other sofa covers are available online as well as in department and bedding stores.

If it's feasible, you can try buying or replacing scratching trees when you replace furniture. Move the furniture around, placing the trees, posts, and pads into areas that will help draw the cat away from the new furniture. For instance, place the best tree nearest to the sofa, a post near a chair, and so on. This will give the cat an area of her own amid her owners, and her own territory to mark. You can cover the furniture until the cat is regularly using her post or tree. Whether you wish to keep it covered or not is your choice. If you wish to remove the cover, do so only when you are there to watch the cat and be sure she does not suddenly "discover" the new furniture. Eventually, when you are sure the cat will stick to her post or tree, you can leave the covers off permanently.

## The Declawing Controversy

Wouldn't it be easier just to get your cat declawed? Declawing, simply stated, is the surgical removal of the last bone of each toe, which includes the claws, either on the front feet alone (which is the most common) or of the front and hind feet. Technically speaking, its surgery, called onychectomy, in which the cat is put under anesthesia and the claws, as well as the cells that promote claw growth, and the third phalanx (the last of the three toe bones) are removed. Afterward, the area is stitched and the cat goes home after an overnight stay in the hospital.

There is quite a controversy about whether declawing is a cruel form of mutilation. Some say it is better to declaw than to get rid of a cat who insists on scratching up the house. There is a point here, but the effects on the cat of declawing should be considered carefully.

Despite some opinions and studies to the contrary, some cats have developed severe behavioral problems due to declawing. What happens is that the pain from the surgery makes the cat's feet hurt, especially in the litter box. The cat can start to associate the litter box with the pain and will begin to avoid it. In some declawed cats this fear becomes permanent and even retraining does not stop them from avoiding the litter box.

One friend of mine who had her first cat declawed vowed never to do it again. She said her cat was in pain for weeks and refused to use the litter box; her feet became sensitive and the cat was visibly stressed. Although the average time for recovery after declawing is three days, often it takes longer.

There is, however, a brand new type of declawing surgery that has only recently become affordable enough for veterinary hospitals to use. Laser declawing uses lasers rather than a scalpel to do the operation. The procedure is the same, but the laser heals small vessels and nerves as it cuts, keeping bleeding to a minimum, and probably pain as well.

A cat who has been declawed does know that her claws are no longer there. Some declawed cats resort to biting and using their teeth, since their ultimate defense weapon, their claws, is not there to assist them. When trying to stretch, a declawed cat cannot dig in and anchor herself, as a cat with claws can. Grooming and scratching are affected, as is the cat's balance when leaping.

In many parts of Europe it is illegal to declaw cats, and some veterinarians in the United States refuse to perform the operation. Declawing is also a no-no in most cat registries. Many cat shelters have a strict no-declawing policy (as well as a must-be-kept-indoors policy) for the cats they adopt out.

On the other hand, some cats do just fine and show very little, if any, effects from the procedure once their feet have healed. Some owners of declawed cats who have had no problems with the procedure claim that the surgery improved their attitude toward their cat. Since the cat was no longer clawing up the furniture, the owner was happier and the relationship between cat and owner improved. Some apartment complexes fear destruction of their property and

**Online Resources**

For more on declawing, please visit this excellent Web site that illustrates this procedure with graphics:

www.maxshouse.com/facts_
about_declawing.htm

will be reluctant to rent to owners of cats with full claws intact.

Kittens do much better with declawing than adult cats. So much so that most veterinarians will not recommend or even perform declawing on an adult cat (over 6 months of age). Adult cats simply do not recover as well, and many will experience recurring pain throughout their life.

Since there is no way of knowing beforehand whether your cat will be affected long term by this surgery, declawing should be done only as a last resort and only if absolutely necessary. Talk to your veterinarian before taking this step and, as with any big decision, think it through carefully. When trained properly, almost any cat will happily use a scratching post or tree. In most of the cases I have seen, the owners either gave up too soon, not wanting to take the time to train their cat, or they declawed the cat without trying at all.

## Other Alternatives

Besides declawing, there are other ways to stop a stubborn scratcher from damaging your property. One is keeping the cat's nails clipped. This will not stop your cat from scratching, but any damage will be greatly minimized.

The only problem with this is that most cats hate to have their paws held while their nails are clipped. As with all training, starting with a kitten is easier. If you get your cat accustomed to having her paws held at a young age, and work your way up to nail clipping, often

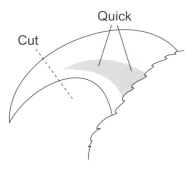

Cut on the line, making sure to avoid the quick.

the cat will learn to accept it and possibly even enjoy the attention.

Hold the cat's or kitten's paws gently and rub softly, allowing the cat to get used to the feeling. Never force the cat to hold her paws still. If she wants to go, let her go. Talk softly and let your cat know that this is a great experience to be loved and enjoyed. Often, choosing a time when the cat is most relaxed, such as when she's in your lap, will create a more positive atmosphere for the cat to learn to relax during this experience.

When your cat or kitten is comfortable with paw-holding, it's time to try clipping a few nails. Clippers made for cats work best. Expose the claw gently by holding the paw and putting light pressure on the top and bottom of the paw, just near the claw, until the claw is completely visible. Snip the end of the nail, being careful not to cut the quick (the pink vein inside the claw). It may take several tries over a couple of days to cut all the claws, because if your cat gets frightened, it is best to stop and wait. Keep working with the cat and be positive about it.

This method has worked with most of my cats. All accept having their paws held, but a couple still refuse to have their claws clipped. The moment the clippers come into view, suddenly they forget that they love the attention of having their paws held. With these cats, often I must catch them while they are in a sound sleep and only do one or two nails at a time—they generally wake after the first or second nail and catch on. Oh well, you can't win them all!

## Nail Covers

Developed by Dr. Toby Wexler of Lafayette, Louisiana, Soft Paws are soft vinyl caps that fit over each nail, almost like false nails for a person. With her nails safely covered, the cat can still indulge in scratching behavior without damaging to the furniture. Soft Paws are available commercially, or you can ask your veterinarian for more information about them.

**Online Resources**

To learn more about Soft Paws and nail trimming, check out:

www.maxshouse.com/ Claw%20Trimming.htm

Working with your cat to correct inappropriate behavior will bring the two of you closer, as long as you use plenty of love and patience. In the long run, the time spent getting to know your cat and the results of better behavior will ensure a closer relationship between the two of you.

# 6

# Cat Hair Everywhere

Once again Mr. Taylor coughed as he swallowed a few strands of long black fur. He gazed over at the cat sitting by the refrigerator staring at him as if expecting to be fed—again! Why did Blacky's fur fall out so much, and how could he stop having to sit in it, eat it, drink it, and sleep in it? His wife vacuumed the house daily. Yet he could make a whole new cat out of the fur he pulled off his clothes and furniture every day.

If you have a cat, chances are you're finding cat hair in your morning coffee, on your work clothes, in your bed. Basically, everywhere. Having an indoor cat, or more than one indoor cat, means more cat hair around the house than you would have with a cat who spends most or all of his time outdoors. But cat hair doesn't have to drive you crazy. In this chapter I'm going to discuss helpful hints on keeping it in check, and also ways to clean up other little kitty messes that can occur with an indoor cat.

## The Cat's Coat

In nature, a cat's coat is useful for many purposes, such as keeping the cat warm, protecting him from the elements, and even camouflage.

Generally, there are three types of hair that make up the cat's coat. For warmth, the cat has two layers of fur: the soft, thick down hairs, which are short and grow close to the skin; and the awn hairs, which are slightly longer and stiffer. The guard hairs, which form the top layer of fur, provide camouflage and protect the awn and down hairs from the elements.

On every cat, these layers vary in length and thickness. All three layers on a longhaired cat are longer and thicker than they are on a shorthaired cat. With the advent of breeding and domesticity came still more variation in coats and colors. Not only are there cats with long hair and short hair, but now there are also cats with short, curly coats (Rex cats), and even almost bald cats, such as the Sphynx, who have very soft down hairs that are almost invisible.

Regardless of whether the coat is long or short, most cats go through coat changes, particularly in the spring and fall, when one type of coat is shed and another replaces it. In nature, and with cats who are frequently outdoors, these changes are more prevalent as the daylight time varies, not (as may seem the case) when the weather changes. But since indoor-only cats are constantly exposed to artificial light, most of them shed year round.

Unfortunately, all this cat hair ends up everywhere—on your sofa, in your food, on your clothes, on the floor, on the drapes. The more cats you have, the more cat hair you have around the house. For allergy sufferers, this can be a problem (though it's the dander and not the actual hair that triggers allergies).

Cat hair is not just annoying, it can be damaging, too. More than once we have had the furnace repairman here to fix a problem that was largely due to cat hair clogging the motor. Electronic equipment can easily be ruined by cat hair. VCRs, televisions, and computer drives can all get clogged with cat hair and can cost a lot of money to fix. Although you can't rid your home completely of hair, you can control it and keep it from damaging your property. There are several ways to do this, the first of which starts with your cat.

# Grooming

Anyone who owns a cat has seen the process by which they groom themselves. Short, backward spikes on a cat's tongue enable them to comb through their fur, pulling debris, parasites, and loose hairs from their coat. By pulling and rearranging the hairs during grooming, a cat also helps regulate his body temperature. The grooming process also keeps the cat's coat healthy by stimulating the sebum glands, which are located at the base of each hair. These glands are responsible for the oils that lubricate and waterproof the fur.

Most cats do an excellent job of keeping themselves clean. Indoor cats tend to be much cleaner than their outdoor counterparts, simply because they are exposed to less dirt and have more leisure time for grooming. Still, all cats, whether longhair, shorthair, or even bald, should be regularly brushed or combed in one way or another. Of course, the longer the cat's coat, the more often this needs to be done, but every cat benefits from it, and so will you.

Since cats are so wonderful at keeping themselves groomed, you may be wondering why you should bother stepping in at all. But the fact of the matter is that there are reasons why you should help your cat in his grooming process.

For one thing, look at all the hair that ends up in your brush when you groom the cat—this means there's that much less hair on the sofa and around the house. Also, the more you help your cat to rid himself of that loose fur, the less likely your cat will be to have hairballs (those horrible little matted wads of fur that cats swallow when they groom, then later vomit onto your beautiful carpet). That helps not only you, but the cat as well, as hairballs can sometimes cause blockages in a cat's intestines if they become too large.

Your cat's coat and how well the cat keeps it groomed can also tell you a lot about the health and well-being of your beloved pet. A dull coat, excessive shedding, bald patches, or lesions can be signs that something is really wrong and your cat needs to see the veterinarian.

Grooming your cat will also help strengthen the bond between cat and owner. Most cats, if properly introduced to it, will enjoy regular grooming. This will give your cat and you something to look forward to and share.

## Grooming the Longhaired Cat

Sammy has an unusually soft, thick undercoat that is plush and soft, and guard hairs that are long and beautiful. Everyone who touches him marvels at his clean, well-kept coat. His fur is like very soft cotton. In the summer, as with any longhaired cat, it mats more quickly due to the humid air and he needs more brushing than in the winter. I brush him every day, though, and he doesn't get any mats, even in the summer.

I also have a purebred Himalayan. Mikai's fur is thick and mats so easily that I cannot keep up with it. Show cats of this quality have to be regularly groomed, often professionally, brushed daily and bathed before shows. Detangling conditioners and sprays help keep their coats gorgeous. But Mikai is not a show cat and I haven't the time to devote to the grooming she requires. She is also quite uncomfortable in the summer, even though we live in a basement apartment that is cool all year round. And so, every June Mikai takes a trip to the

*A coat like Mikai's needs a great deal of grooming.*

*After being clipped every summer, Mikai is much happier and
more comfortable.*

groomer, where she is given what is called a kitten clip. Her fur is
clipped down short, except her tail, legs, and head, which are washed
and brushed out. It lasts all summer, keeps her cool, and no mats form
(they don't ever form on her tail). She is always happiest after her kitten clip. She purrs more and is more active and playful. By fall, her
coat has grown back out in all its beauty and is easier to care for
because it doesn't mat as easily.

It is your choice whether you wish to groom your cat yourself, have
a professional bathe and brush him, or have him clipped as I do with
Mikai. If you wish to do your own brushing, it is best to start when
your cat is a kitten. If you acclimate your kitten from the start to
being brushed, making it a positive experience, chances are very
good he will grow up looking forward to being brushed.

Sammy loves the slicker brush (the kind with a flat head and thin,
bent pins). If he sees me lift it up, he begins to purr and struts over,
rubbing his face against the brush. This is the attitude you want from
your cat. But even if you adopt an adult longhaired cat, you can still
teach him to accept grooming by brushing him regularly, giving him

treats while you do it, making it a fun experience, and never forcing the cat to stay or do anything he does not wish to do. The moment you start to force the cat to remain when he wishes to go, you have begun a cycle of grooming failure.

I use a slicker brush because the stiff bristles rake the fur, helping to prevent mats from forming. But this may not be the best brush to start with if your cat or kitten is not used to being brushed. Buy a soft-bristled brush and work slowly up to a slicker.

Be gentle when brushing, no matter what type of brush you use. Don't tear at the fur, as this can be painful and give the cat a bad impression of brushing. When I was first getting Sammy accustomed to a daily routine of brushing, I would brush only the top part of the hair, gradually and gently working the brush deeper into his fur. He grew to love the attention, and your cat probably will, too.

Longhaired cats should be brushed several times a week—more in spring and summer when the coat is changing to a lighter one (even indoor cats have winter and summer coats; they are just not as prominent as cats outdoors in areas with drastic seasonal changes).

You can also use a comb on your cat (flea combs work well for grooming, but there are grooming combs as well), particularly if the coat is thick. I find that flea combs, with their closer teeth, are better at parting the hairs and preventing mats. As with brushing, be careful not to pull at the fur and cause your cat pain. Use a comb to get at the areas on the head and around the face, avoiding the cat's eyes, ears, and mouth (and don't get the comb caught on those whiskers). Work your way down the cat's back and tail, and be sure to get underneath as well. Mats tend to form most readily under the cat's arms, between his legs, on his belly, and behind his ears, so pay special attention to those areas.

Sammy is unusual in that he does not mind me brushing his rear area and underneath him. Usually, he'll just roll over for me. When he's not in the mood to roll over, I lift his front legs up with one hand while combing or brushing underneath. Usually a cat will only tolerate this for a very short time, however, so work carefully but quickly. Again, don't force your cat to remain there if he does not want to.

Brushing, although it helps remove many dead hairs, only loosens even more hair that the cat licks off or that falls to the floor. To avoid this, end each grooming session by quickly wiping your cat with a moistened towel or even antished-

**Online Resources**

For more on antishedding wipes, go to:

www.simplesolution.com

ding wipes that can be found in the pet supply store. These wipes are made to reduce nonessential shedding, yet they don't interfere with the seasonal shedding process. They are premoistened and can be used on dry coats as well as wet.

A couple of haircuts for longhaired cats, one called a lion clip and another called a kitten clip, can be done by groomers to keep shedding down and make brushing less of a duty (though still a necessity).

### Dematting

There are times when mats just seem to form, even with regular brushing. A mat will be easier to remove the sooner you catch it. And it must be removed, because mats will just get bigger and bigger, eventually pinching painfully at your cat's skin.

Be careful not to pull at mats when you brush or comb your cat. If you come across a small mat, grasp it near the base, closest to the cat's skin. Starting at the top part of the mat farthest from the cat's skin, work the comb through the mat using sweeping motions. Make sure you keep a firm enough grasp on the base of the mat to prevent any pulling on the cat's skin. Work your way up the mat slowly, until you have worked through the entire mat.

Detangling sprays and conditioners soften the mat and help the comb work through it. Special detangling powders made for cats can be sprinkled on the mat as well, and can aid in combing it out more easily. There are also combs that are specifically made to remove mats.

If a mat is too large or too tight to be combed out, you can clip it by using blunt-edged scissors. Be careful not to touch the skin when you clip.

*Leave It to the Pros*

If your longhaired cat develops mats that are large, numerous, and/or close to the skin, you should let a professional groomer deal with them rather than trying to take care of things yourself. Often the cat will need to have the mats shaved off and the rest of the coat bathed to get rid of small mats and prevent further matting.

## Grooming the Shorthaired Cat

Shorthaired cats need to be groomed, too. They also shed, get hair all over the house, and develop hair balls. Brush your cat once a week, if you can.

For shorthairs, a soft-bristled brush is fine. After brushing, comb the cat to catch any hair the soft brush loosened. Follow with a nice run-over with a chamois cloth, and your shorthaired cat will remain slick and beautiful.

# Bathing a Cat

Most indoor cats never need to be bathed. Unlike outdoor cats, indoor cats rarely get into anything dangerous or that they can't wash off on their own. But there may be times when your cat needs your help to get really clean.

Show cats are regularly bathed to keep their coats in top condition. Besides aiding in the health of the coat and controlling shedding, bathing may be required if parasites are present and a flea bath is needed. Some smaller mats can be removed more easily if the cat is bathed and a dematting shampoo or conditioner is used. A case of excessive diarrhea can cause a longhaired cat to become messy and require bathing. If your cat gets a toxic substance on his fur, or gets into something so dirty that he cannot clean it off himself, he will require a bath as well.

But cats hate water, right? Well, for the most part, yes. Gentleness and patience are the keys, particularly for a cat who reacts violently to being bathed.

Before beginning the cat's bath, make sure everything is ready and within reach beside the sink or tub where the bathing will be done. Prepare the following items:

- Soft bath towel (preferably terrycloth)
- Washcloth
- Shampoo specifically for cats
- Tearless baby shampoo
- A towel or mat for the bottom of the sink
- Cotton balls

Where you choose to bathe the cat depends on you. Many people prefer to use a sink equipped with a spray hose attachment. This is a good idea, as the nozzle can be held against the cat's skin, reducing the noise of running water, which frightens many cats. Other people like to "suffer" with their cat by running bath water in the tub and getting in with the cat. Also available commercially are small tubs made just for cats that hold the cat in place, enabling you to have both hands free to concentrate on bathing.

However you choose to do it, make sure it is most comfortable and calming for the cat. For the purpose of simplicity, I'm going explain a bath as given in a sink. You can modify the information for your own convenience and preferences.

Before beginning, place a mat or towel at the bottom of the sink. This will help keep your cat from slipping around, which could cause him more fear. Fill the sink with an inch or two of water and adjust the water temperature. You want the water to be warm, not too hot and not cold.

It is advisable to clip your cat's nails beforehand to help avoid painful scratches. Next, thoroughly brush the coat to remove loose hairs. Be gentle and calm. Place cotton balls in the cat's ears. This will help to keep out the shampoo. Some cats, however, will not tolerate this, and it will only make matters worse—don't force the issue. If this is the case, be extra careful when washing your cat's head.

If you can get an assistant to help hold your cat during the bath, great. If not, be careful, especially if your cat is not accustomed to baths. You may want to wear protective gloves.

Place your cat in the sink, holding his scruff with a firm grip and with his back facing you. Wet the cat thoroughly with the nozzle of the hose or with a container of warm water (don't push your cat under a running faucet), making sure you get all the way to the skin. Try to eliminate splashing sounds (that may frighten the cat more) by holding the nozzle or opening of the container gently against the cat's body. Do not spray the head or face, because this too can cause a panic. Use the washcloth to dab small amounts of water around the cat's face.

Once the cat is thoroughly soaked, take a handful of cat shampoo and run it through the coat, rubbing it in and creating a good lather. Don't forget to get the cat's belly and tail. Speak to your cat in a soothing tone to show him this is not a punishment.

Place a tiny amount of no-tear baby shampoo on the washcloth and carefully wash the cat's face. Use just one finger rather than your whole hand, as this will make it easier to get around the eyes, ears, and mouth.

When the cat is thoroughly washed, rinse with the spray nozzle as before. Rinse his face using the washcloth. *Never* spray water in a cat's face. Once all traces of the shampoo are removed from the coat, you may use a conditioner made for cats, if you wish. Rinse thoroughly.

 **Online Resources**

To learn more about bathing a cat:

> www.neko.mi.org/~tawollen/
> humor/msg00361.html
>
> www.peninsulahumane
> society.org/resource/
> column2-52.html
>
> www.petplace.com/
> articles/artShow
> .asp?artID=1377

When done, wrap your wet kitty in the terrycloth towel and keep him warm. Don't allow any drafts or chills to get to the cat.

After a good towel-drying, comb the cat's fur carefully to prevent matting, particularly with longhairs. You may blow-dry the cat if he is willing, but be careful not to get the blow dryer too close to the skin and keep it on a low setting. Brush the fur backward as well as forward using a slicker brush as you blow-dry. Blow-drying is best done on longhaired cats to keep the coat fluffy.

Remember to keep your patience throughout the entire process to help keep your cat as calm as possible.

If your cat simply will not allow you to bathe him, no matter what method you use to restrain him or how calm you are about the whole thing, you can use a dry or self-rinsing shampoo. Ring 5 has a good self-rinsing shampoo called Quick Clean that is good for an on-the-spot cleaning.

## A Healthy Coat

Keeping your cat in top condition will keep his coat healthy and prevent excessive shedding. Shedding is a natural process, but can be lessened if the skin is healthy. Excessive shedding is sometimes a sign of poor health in general or skin health in particular. Some cats do have poorer skin health than others and do shed more. By correcting general health and skin conditions, these can be minimized.

Excessive shedding and dandruff can also be a sign that something is missing in the cat's diet. Mineral oil in the cat's food will help combat dandruff and dry skin, which will, in turn, aid in preventing excessive shedding.

## Home Sweet Cat Home

Besides grooming, bathing, brushing, and keeping your cat healthy, the other way to minimize cat hair in your home is through general cleanliness and by using a few simple tricks that will make cleanup in your home simpler. This may sound like a lot of work, but it doesn't have to be. Ten or fifteen minutes a day is all it takes to keep cat hair from carpeting your home.

Vacuuming may seem the obvious way to keep cat hair picked up, and in general it is. Upright vacuums work deep into the pile of the carpet, and many brands are now equipped with HEPA (high efficiency particulate air) filters that keep out allergens and extra dust.

Vacuuming should be done every day, particularly in multicat households, to keep cat hair to a minimum. But vacuuming the carpet alone won't get it all. As I learned, cat hair gets into everything, including furnaces and electronics. If your cat spends a good amount of time near your furnace, you might want to vacuum around it to keep cat hair away. I usually remove the door to the furnace and vacuum around the motor once a week. Also vacuum around your computer equipment, behind the refrigerator, and around fans, air conditioners, televisions, VCRs, and other electronics regularly.

Those little tumbleweeds of hair that blow by your feet and lodge in the radiator can be cleaned up during on-the-spot cleaning using a hand vac, if you have one.

Vacuuming alone can't get cat hair out of everything, however. Even though my cats are never in my car unless they are confined to a carrier, my car seats, being cloth, are still covered with a fuzzy layer. This is from the fur that sticks to my clothes, which is transferred to the cloth of the car seats. To clean them, I generally run my hand along the layer of fur, rolling it into a ball and loosening it. I vacuum those hair balls, then use a lint brush to loosen and remove what is left. The same method can be used on sofas and chairs.

A strip of masking tape, sticky side out, can be wrapped around your hand to remove hair from clothes and even furniture. You can buy rolls of a sticky paper that is used the same way. A damp sponge wiped across your couch will also roll the hair into little balls that are easily removed. Or you can buy a pet hair remover sponge. These are different than "ordinary" sponges. As you wipe the sponge across the surface of the furniture, the fur is rolled into a ball you can then easily pick up or vacuum.

As for furniture, cat owners often find that furnishings made from wood, metal, plastic, and ceramics are the easiest to keep clean in a cat-filled home.

Sofa covers, washable cushion covers, and chair covers are not only attractive, but will keep cat hair off your furniture, and they can

## The Light Shedders

If you want to avoid cat hair for the most part and still have a cat or two, there are several breeds of cats who shed very little. The curly coated Cornish Rex has a coat of tight hair that sheds very little. The Sphynx, as I mentioned earlier, has almost no hair at all. But these cats need to be kept warm constantly.

I have heard that the Bengal and the Singapura, although they have beautiful coats, are light shedders. If you are interested in any of these cats, I would advise visiting a cat show and speaking to breeders, or asking your veterinarian if he or she knows of a breeder in your area who specializes in these cats.

simply be thrown into the washing machine. On the same note, towels and cat beds can be placed in the locations your cat prefers to sleep, which will be where the most cat hair will accumulate. Choosing furniture with patterns or in darker shades will make cat hair less noticeable. If you have one cat or even two cats of basically the same color, you can choose covers or even furniture to match the cat.

Houses with many cats obviously have more of a problem with cat hair than those with one or two cats. Hardwood floors coated with polyurethane and area rugs are easier to keep clean in multicat households than is wall-to-wall carpeting. Dusters that use a magnetic material to attract dust and debris work quite well, but have to be replaced regularly. These dusters also pick up cat hair, and they are great for cleaning around valuables and in hard-to-reach areas.

Electronic air filters not only keep the indoor environment fresh and clean, they can also help keep cat hair and dander down, which benefits allergy sufferers. Many are also equipped with HEPA filters and other allergy fighters. If you have mild allergies and think you can't have a cat or two, try one of these air-filtration systems.

## Other Cat Messes

Owning a cat means hair is not the only thing you'll have to clean up. Other little messes will invariably be left around the house from time to time, regardless of the breed of cat you choose. Those hairballs get coughed up onto your sofa or carpet, or the cat misses his litter box or chooses another area to relieve himself for whatever reason.

To remove a coughed-up hairball or the product of a dinner eaten too fast, pick up whatever mess you can with a paper towel, then sprinkle baking soda on the area, leaving it there until it dries. Once it's hard and crumbly, the baking soda can be removed with a vacuum cleaner, hand vac, or dustpan and broom. The baking soda soaks up any moisture that is left after the mess is picked up with a paper towel. A squirt of Resolve Carpet Cleaner and a slightly damp rag run over the area will take care of anything that may be left behind.

Litter box lapses can be cleaned using the same method with one variation. Since you don't want the cat returning to that spot, after blotting away the moisture with a paper towel, pour an enzymatic cleaner that breaks down organic matter onto the area. The baking soda can be sprinkled on afterward, and when all is cleaned up, the lack of odor should prevent the cat from returning.

Keep the area covered until it's dry. Try taping something that the cat finds unpleasant over the area: double-sided tape, aluminum foil, or one of those office floor mats with the spiked side up. Besides cleaning the area, you can use a carpet deodorizer regularly when vacuuming to cover any surface odors.

### 🖱 Online Resources

The following is a list of sites featuring odor-control products that are especially good at helping to eliminate pet odors:

> www.cleartheair.com/
> www.online-pet-medications.com/pet_odor_control.asp
> www.krystal-air.com/Pets/pets.htm
> www.ecochem.com/t_cbpet.html
> www.odordestroyer.com/

Use a dust-free litter and locate the box on an easily cleanable surface to keep down tracking and dust in the air. For more information on litter box problems and solutions, see chapter 4.

## Safe Cleaning

Beware of cleaning your cat's eating and sleeping spots with chemicals that may be harmful to the cat, such as anything that contains tar, coal, carbolic acid, wool tar, or cresol.

Feed your cats on a mat using nontippable dishes (ceramic bowls are good, or weighted stainless steel) and on a cleanable surface. Cat food cans should be rinsed out before being put in the recycle bin or thrown in the garbage, so that they don't stink up the house.

# 7

# The Outdoor Indoor Cat

**M**iss Jones was distraught. Her cat, Timothy, who had never been outside in his life, had slipped out a door that stuck open after a repairman left the house. The 6-year-old tabby had been missing for days, and Miss Jones was sure she would never see her beloved cat again.

But then one night, as if it was a miracle, Miss Jones looked out her window and there stood Timothy waiting at the door as if this was his daily routine. She was so happy to have him home, and he settled back in as if nothing had happened—at first.

Two weeks later, Timothy was staring at the door as if he was waiting for it to open, or looking for a way to open it himself. Miss Jones lived near a busy highway. She didn't want to risk Timothy getting out again. But what could she do? How could she satisfy Timothy and allow him outdoors without endangering his life?

Cats love basking in the sunshine, sniffing the fresh air, and watching butterflies. Just because your cat is indoors all the time does not mean she can't enjoy these pleasures. There are options available to

KARA LEE LODOLCE

*Just because a cat is an indoor cat does not mean she cannot safely go outside. This kitty is wearing a Cat Walking Jacket and is having a wonderful time in the grass.*

the indoor-only cat owner who wants their cat to continue enjoying a romp in the sunshine. Which option is right for you will depend on the cat's personality, your finances, and where you live. Certain situations (if you're renting your home, for example) may limit which options you can choose, but there are always other options available.

## Outdoor Enclosures

If you own your home or have permission to build on your property and have a little imagination and some building skills, you can create an efficient and attractive outdoor enclosure for your cat(s). Even if you don't have the building skills or the money to afford carpenters, you can still provide an outdoor enclosure for your cat's fun and safety.

The options are limitless when you set out to build your cat's enclosure. It can be a structure as simple as a small chain-link run or as elaborate as an entirely fenced yard. You can build an access door to the enclosure using a cat door or a window. Just remember that every outdoor enclosure must have a sunny place for basking, a shady place for cooling down, and a fresh supply of water.

## Do Fence Me In

There are premade chain-link enclosures available for anyone looking for an easy and quick backyard run for their cats. Sears sells eight-foot exercise pens, which are a good start for your cat's outdoor

*Cat enclosures can be custom built of chain-link fencing, giving your cat plenty of room to stretch and play.*

excursions. Make sure you buy (or build) a chain-link enclosure that is escape-proof. That means no gaps the cat can slip under or through, and all sides enclosed, including the top.

A chain-link enclosure can include perches and extra additions, or you can build your own. Adding a tree, plants (nonpoisonous), and toys will help make this enclosure an ideal escape for your cat.

## Porch, Patio, or Balcony

Another simple yet effective idea is to screen in an already-existing porch, patio, or balcony. You might want to build runs, ramps, or climbing trees in the screened area for your cat's amusement. I screened in my porch for my cats, and they love to sleep in the sun on the shelves I built within it. A few plants or trees in pots around the patio will turn it into a cat garden and give your cat a feel for the outdoors, plants to hide in, bugs to chase, and sunshine to enjoy.

### Mesh Cat Enclosures

Mesh enclosures are just now becoming popular. Made of durable nylon mesh that can't be shredded by cat claws, these enclosures can provide your cat with fun and varied surroundings. The catalog company Doctors Foster & Smith offers a variety of fantastic mesh cat enclosures for a reasonable price. You can start out with the Kittywalk Deck & Patio, which is an all-mesh "run" you can place on a deck or patio and doesn't require staking to the ground. If you want to get more elaborate, you can purchase Kitty's Room, which is basically a tent that you can add to the Kittywalk. It gives your cat a place to hide or to just get out of the sunshine. You can place her food and water bowls inside. The Kittywalk Penthouse is five feet tall and includes a sunshade and three hammocks at different levels for puss to lounge on. It's made of collapsible netting and a sturdy metal frame. To see other Kittywalk products, visit www.DrsFosterSmith.com or call (800) 381-7179.

But be extra careful to secure the screening around any balcony, especially on upper floors, to prevent falls. Even for agile cats, falls can be fatal.

## Other Ideas

If you wish to get more elaborate, simple chicken wire and wood can be turned into many interesting feline play areas. Tarps can be used to cover part of an enclosure for shade, ramps can be built for climbing, and trees may be added.

Not too long ago, a friend showed me pictures of an outdoor enclosure a relative had built for her cats. It was constructed like a small house, screened in and done up in white painted wood. The shingled roof kept out rain. Inside were not only shelves and ramps, but cat trees, a litter box, and lots of places to play. A tube ran from a basement window into the enclosure, so the cats could get to it from the house with ease and the owners did not have to worry about rain, wind, or unwelcome critters entering.

A fenced yard can also be made a safe haven for cats. The fence should have a small-enough mesh so the cats cannot escape through it (stockade fencing is ideal) and be sunk into the ground so they cannot get under it. The fence should be at least six feet high, and chicken wire or metal can be placed horizontally over the top of the fence to prevent the cats from escaping over it. It can also be placed over treetops to keep the cats from climbing the trees and getting over the fence.

There are disadvantages to outdoor enclosures, however, and you should be aware of these so they can be avoided. Make sure your cat always has access to the indoors whenever she wants. During inclement weather, your cat may not want to be exposed to the elements and will need to get inside, even if you are not around to let her in.

Also, a cat who goes outdoors is exposed to pests and parasites such as fleas, ticks, worms, snakes, and dangerous insects. Keep any runs or enclosures sprayed with a vet-approved yard spray. With a little care and caution, your indoor cat can enjoy a safe time and still reap the benefits of outdoor exercise.

# Bringing the Outdoors Indoors

If you don't have a backyard or even a terrace or porch, there are still things you can do to help your cat enjoy the delights of sunshine, fresh air, and a sense of the wild life.

## Window Perches and Boxes

Window perches or boxes are inexpensive and simple ways for your cat to enjoy the fresh air and sunshine, although they do not provide the freedom to run. However, most cats will still enjoy just being able to lie in the sunshine and smell the fresh air. Perches provide a wide, soft bed that clips right onto your windowsill. Window boxes are securely screened boxes that fit into an open window, like the housing for a large air conditioner.

## Indoor Gardens

If you have a green thumb and a love of cats, the two can be combined to make a cat-friendly solarium or indoor garden. This sounds like something only the wealthy would have, but a garden can be modified to fit almost any house or even apartment (if the landlord will allow it). A garden or solarium can be almost any size and can be built on a screened or glassed porch or in a sunny room. A small garden can even be created on or near a windowsill.

Since this is for your cat's benefit, any plants in the garden should be cat-friendly. Plants such as grasses, valerian, cat mint, cat thyme, Japanese matatabi, clover, and catnip are examples of plants cats enjoy, and some can be dried to make homemade cat toys.

Since cats love to use dirt as a commode, you may want to cover the exposed soil with chicken wire or something more attractive, such as gravel or pinecones.

# Leash Training

Yes, cats can be trained to walk on a leash. They will not, however, heel by your side as a dog will. But with proper introductions, training, and acclimation, you can take your cat outside safely with you in control.

# Chicago Public Library
## Humboldt Park
2/22/2017   3:37:12 PM
-Patron Receipt-

## ITEMS BORROWED:

1:
Title: The house of a million pets/
Item #: R0604690748
Due Date: 3/15/2017

2:
Title: The Cat Fanciers Association comple
Item #: R0403015333
Due Date: 3/15/2017

---

## Warning!

*Never* tie your cat on a line outside and leave her all alone. The cat will be vulnerable to other animals and to the weather. Also, even when you are around, don't put the line near a tree that the cat can climb up and then get the leash or rope caught.

---

Before I explain the basic steps, there are a few warnings about leash training. First and foremost is always to use a harness specifically made for cats. Never use a collar, as it can slip off the cat's neck or may strangle her. One other caution to leash training is that many cats, once taught to go outside, will continue to want to go out even if you are not in the mood for a walk. They learn quickly where the door is and may slip out unexpectedly—without the leash. Taking the cat out in a carrier (with harness on) or through a different door than the one that is used for people may help prevent this.

Harnesses for cats come in three basic styles: the figure-8, the H, and the V styles. The figure-8 harness is one of the best for walks outside, since it tightens a bit if the cat pulls, preventing the cat from slipping out.

The leash should be of a lightweight material, not a big, bulky kind you would buy for a dog. You can get a leash and harness that match. There are also harnesses in which the leash and harness are all one unit.

Following are the basic steps for training your cat to walk on a leash. It is best to start when the cat is young, but an older cat can learn, too. It is also important to make sure the harness you use is the proper size and is placed on the animal correctly. You should be able to slip two fingers between the cat and the harness when it is in place. To get a harness that fits your cat properly, take your cat with you when you buy it, if you can.

## Step One

Familiarize the cat or kitten with the equipment. Place the harness and leash on the floor in front of your cat and allow her to inspect them. Using the leash like a toy, play with the cat by dragging the leash along the floor like a string. Make the leash a fun item, something to enjoy.

## Step Two

Once your cat or kitten has become familiar with the harness and leash, slip on the harness on and buckle it, but do not hook the leash on yet. Let your cat get accustomed to the feel of the harness by itself.

Some cats will act as if you have just put some horrible restraining device on them and will roll around and try to get it off. If your cat acts this way, do not take the harness off. If you do, the cat will only learn that this behavior is rewarded by removal of the offending harness. Instead, distract the cat with play or a treat.

Do not leave the cat alone while she's in the harness. Keep watch until she begins to calm down. Once your cat has relaxed, take the harness off.

---

### Safety Katz Walking Jacket

Does your cat hate wearing a store-bought harness? Perhaps she will prefer a walking jacket. Designed by Neta Doyle and her daughter, these jackets are made to fit almost any size kitty, from your wee kitten to your wannabe lion. All you need to do is measure your cat's neck and chest and choose the jacket that best fits her. For information, sizes, prices, and great pictures of cats using their walking jackets, visit www.joykatz.net/walkingjackets.htm, or write to Neta Doyal, 907 S. College, Brady, TX 76825.

---

## Step Three

Continue to place the harness on your cat every day, preferably several times, for longer and longer periods until your cat is completely accustomed to it. Tell the cat how good she is and give her rewards for good behavior.

## Step Four

Next, hook the leash to the harness. Hold the leash loosely and do not drag, pull, or tug at it. Follow your cat around the house, wherever she wants to go. Don't expect your cat to walk at your side like a dog. However, you can help things along by offering food rewards as you walk slowly ahead, enticing the cat to follow.

## Step Five

Once your cat is walking easily with you, it is time to take her outdoors. Be careful where you walk with your cat. It's best to stay away from highways and busy streets, or anywhere there may be aggressive animals or other dangers. Loud noises may frighten your cat, so take her to quiet spots to walk and relax.

Do not let your cat walk on neighbor's lawns or eat grass, because it may have been sprayed with insecticides or lawn chemicals.

Keep in mind that some cats are easier to train than others. Some will take to leash training easily; others may never get accustomed to it. Don't force your cat to walk with you, and never force a shy cat to go outdoors if she doesn't want to. Some cats just do not enjoy being outside—it frightens them. Other cats might become wild or uncontrollable. Some cats simply would rather stay in the house. For these cats, windowsills or screened porches are a better alternative. Know your cat and her reactions, and have a good time in the sunshine with your friend.

# 8

# Your Healthy Cat

A ll the cat knew was that he did not feel well. Something was amiss. But his caretakers did not seem to understand. He cried more often, using a form of verbal communication reserved only for interaction with humans. He did not know what they could do; he only knew that they fed him and cared for his needs, so certainly they would make him feel better. But days went by and he only felt worse. They did not seem to understand why he was crying out to them more. Once in awhile they would speak of him, he would hear his name, or they would look at him with perplexed expressions. But none of this made him feel any better. It wasn't until he could barely stand one day that he was taken to the veterinarian.

## Know Thy Cat

The first step in keeping your cat healthy is to know your cat. You should be in tune with your cat so that you will know when something is wrong. In the wild, small cats are prey animals as well as predators, so it's instinctive for them to hide any obvious signs of trouble for as long as they can. That means what seems to be a minor health problem may already be well on its way to becoming a serious problem. Certain signs can be a warning of an impending health problem in any cat:

- Change in behavior
- Change in appetite
- Increased vocalization
- Increased thirst
- Increased urination
- Vomiting
- Diarrhea
- Constipation

- Depression
- Lack of balance
- Lameness
- Stiff joints
- Coughing
- Sneezing
- Respiratory difficulties
- Runny eyes

These are just some of the changes that may be signs of an ill cat. Knowing your cat well will help you recognize other changes.

## The Home Health Exam

An important part of knowing your cat is performing regular home health exams once a week. These are not difficult to do and will help you spot physical changes you may otherwise have missed. These exams should be done during grooming sessions, and ideally started when your cat is young. (If you've acquired an older cat, please don't skip the exam. It just may take a little time to accustom the cat to the handling.)

When beginning your exam, start by looking at your cat overall. Is his behavior normal? Is he standing and walking properly? Does the cat's balance seem correct? Any noticeable changes should immediately be brought to the attention of your veterinarian.

For the physical exam, you may want to use food treats—and don't forget the praise. Keep your cat calm throughout the exam. If at any time the cat begins to get agitated, it is best to stop and continue at another time when he is more relaxed. Negative associations will only make future exams more difficult, for you as well as the cat.

Start the physical exam with the cat's eyes. They should be bright, clear, and free of excessive discharge. A small amount of clear discharge may be normal, but thick, dark discharge may be the sign of a problem, such as a blocked tear duct or conjunctivitis, and should be brought to the attention of your veterinarian. Check the lenses of your pet's eyes. Do they seem normal? Cloudiness may be a sign of cataracts. Redness or discharge around the lids may mean conjunctivitis.

If your cat bumps into things or seems to have trouble figuring distances, you will want your veterinarian to check his eyesight. When I acquired Teisha, I noticed her movements were slow and cautious. If an object was on the floor that had not been there previously, she would walk into or trip over it. Her pupils dilated normally, but a trip to the veterinarian revealed retinal detachment that caused her blindness.

Next, look into the cat's ears. They should be clean and pink, but not red or swollen. A foul odor is the sign of an ear infection. If the ears look dirty, or if the cat scratches at them continually or shakes his head a lot, ear mites may be present.

Check in the cat's mouth. Most cats resist this, and you will need to be easy and gentle. Place your hand over the cat's head and, using your thumb and middle finger, press lightly on either side of the cat's mouth until he opens it. The gums should be pink, not white, bluish, or yellow.

Lifting one lip carefully and press on the gums. They should turn white at your touch, then quickly return to their natural color. There should be no foul odor from the mouth. This can mean an infection or even kidney or digestive problems. The teeth should be white, not yellow or brown.

Brushing your cat's teeth using a pet toothpaste and finger toothbrush (ask your veterinarian or check the pet supply store) or a baking soda and water mixture is a good idea. Do not use any toothpaste made for humans, as it can make a cat ill.

It's okay if your cat's nose is dry, but there should be no excessive nasal discharge.

Now, feel your way down the cat's body. Start at the neck and throat, feeling for any lumps or sore spots. Check his weight, too. If you can't feel your cat's ribs, it may be time for a diet. On the other hand, if the ribs are sticking out or are more prominent than normal, the cat is losing weight. This could be the indication of a serious health problem.

Next, gently pull up the skin on your cat's neck. The skin should fall right back into place when released. If the skin remains extended, your cat may be dehydrated.

Look through your cat's coat, checking for fleas or other parasites. Flea dirt resembles tiny specks of pepper and turns red when dampened.

Become familiar with your cat's normal pulse rate. Check it for any changes whenever you do his health check. You can feel the pulse by gently pressing right behind the cat's left front leg over the chest area. A normal heart rate is between 140 and 240 beats per minute. Since that is a very wide range, it's important to know what is normal for your cat.

Respiration should be even and barely audible (unless, of course, the cat is purring). Open-mouth breathing, holding the head extended while breathing, or excessive chest movement is abnormal and should be checked by a veterinarian.

Next, run your hand down the cat's legs and paws and feel for any abnormalities (such as swelling, pain, lumps, or stiffness). Also, watch your cat when he walks. Being familiar with his normal gait will help you spot any problem, such as a limp.

Finally, look around your cat's anal area for redness or discharge. If he has tapeworms, they may be visible and will resemble small bits of rice. However, it is still a good practice to have your cat's stool checked for internal parasites whenever he visits the veterinarian.

Cats have anal sacs located on either side of the anus. Occasionally, anal sacs get impacted and may cause irritation. If your cat is scooting his hind end along the floor or licking excessively at his anal area, have a veterinarian check him for impaction.

The entire exam sounds like a lot of work, but once you and your cat become accustomed to the routine of a home health exam it should not take much time at all.

## Neutering Your Cat

I have spoken to people who think that because they are not letting their cat outside where the animal can breed freely, they don't have to have the cat spayed or castrated. Some people cringe at the very idea, as if they will be harming the animal or denying him some fun. But the truth of the matter is that a cat's sexual "desire" is merely instinctual. Cats do not mate for pleasure.

A cat who is not neutered and is kept strictly indoors will drive you crazy trying to get out. Females caterwaul all night when in heat, and males (and even some females) spray foul-smelling urine to advertise their availability. The fact that they are indoors will not change any of these behaviors. Instead, your cat will be frustrated that he cannot fulfill these biological drives.

A cat who is "fixed" is also healthier. Intact cats have a higher incidence of testicular (males) and ovarian and mammary (females) cancer.

Rumors of cats becoming fat and lazy after neutering are myths. As long as you adjust the cat's food intake to meet the slower metabolism and continue with plenty of interaction and play, the cat will remain trim and healthy, and the incessant need to get out of the house to find a mate will diminish. The idea that a female cat must have a litter of kittens before she is spayed is another myth. There is absolutely no physical or behavioral benefit to this, there are many risks, and you are contributing to the cat overpopulation problem, as well.

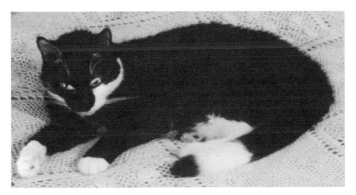

*It is false to assume a cat will become fat and lazy once he is fixed.*

Besides all this, cats who are fixed are more settled and less antsy than cats left intact. So, do your feline friend a favor and have him or her neutered, if possible before sexual maturity sets in (at 5 or 6 months of age).

## Vaccinations

When it comes to indoor cats, vaccines have been a controversial subject for several years. Some veterinarians say if an indoor cat lives in an area where there is no chance of escape and no possibility of other animals coming into the home, then there is no need to vaccinate past kittenhood. Others say annual vaccinations are not necessary, but vaccines at regular intervals are important for an animal's health. Still others insist the old recommendation of annual vaccines is really the only way to be safe. Which vaccines to give is also controversial.

There are valid arguments on every side. The immune system of a cat who is never exposed to any disease is not as strong as one who has had the chance to develop immunities. Therefore, if the cat does become exposed, the chances are higher that he will develop that disease and lower that he will recover. Vaccinating enables the cat to be safely exposed to certain viruses, strengthening the immune system not only against the disease the vaccination protects against, but also in general.

 **Online Resources**

To read the full report on the AAFP/AFM Feline Vaccination Guidelines, visit:

www.aafponline.org

Also, you can carry germs and bacteria into your home on your clothes and shoes. Though it is a lesser risk, some contagious diseases can be transmitted through contact with inanimate objects, such as clothing, luggage, garbage, and food. When your cat licks or sniffs these things, he is exposed to the disease. And if you have other animals in the house coming in and out (such as a dog), there is a chance they could carry viruses or bacteria in with them, even if they are immune.

The law is another good incentive for vaccinating. In Connecticut and many other states, the law says that all cats must be up to date on their rabies vaccinations. It does not matter if the cat is indoors or outdoors, or lives in an apartment or a house.

On the other side of the coin, there are risks involved in vaccinations, and these risks increase as the frequency of the vaccination increases. Gillie came into my life with cancer that was too aggressive to stop. This cancer was vaccination induced, meaning the cancer was related to the annual feline leukemia vaccines he received as an outdoor cat. The shots meant to help save his life took it instead. There are cats who develop tumors on the site of certain vaccinations, most notable feline leukemia and rabies. Sammy developed a small tumor between his shoulder blades from his kitten shots, but the tumor was removed and didn't return.

But do indoor cats really need vaccinations at all (other than rabies if it is the law)? Most vets agree that a kitten needs to have a full series of shots. After that, the decision is split about giving booster shots. It is up to you and your cat's veterinarian to make the final decision.

In 2000 the American Association of Feline Practitioners and the Academy of Feline Medicine released Feline Vaccination Guidelines that have helped cat owners and veterinarians sort though much of the controversy and conflicting information. The guidelines designate four feline vaccines as core, or essential, because of the serious nature of the diseases and the proven efficacy of the vaccine. These are feline panleukopenia (FPV, also known as feline distemper or feline infectious enteritis), feline viral rhinotracheitis (FVR), feline calicivirus (FCV), and rabies. The general recommendations for the core vaccines (except rabies, for which you must follow local laws) are:

- Vaccinate kittens when they first visit the veterinarian at 6 to 8 weeks old.
- Vaccinate again when the kitten is 12 weeks old.
- Give a booster shot when the cat is 1 year old.
- Give a subsequent booster shot every three years, unless there are risk factors that make it necessary to vaccinate more or less often.

Noncore vaccines should only be considered for those cats who risk exposure to a particular disease. They include those against chlamydia, feline leukemia virus (FeLV), feline infectious peritonitis (FIP), bordetella, ringworm, feline immunodeficiency virus (FIV), and giardia.

# Common Ailments

Although indoor cats are generally healthier than outdoor cats, like humans, cats do get sick once in awhile. The following is a basic list of some of the more common health problems that can affect your cat.

## Coughing

If your cat develops a cough, he should be taken to the veterinarian to determine the cause. The most common reason for coughing is hairballs. Never give your cat human cough medicines, as they may contain chemicals that can do more harm than good. Your veterinarian can recommend the best medicine for the problem.

## Diarrhea

Diarrhea can have a variety of causes, from intestinal parasites or food intolerance to serious liver or kidney disease. Two safe and often-recommended medicines to use for mild cases are Kaopectate and Immodium A-D. Consult your veterinarian for the proper dosage. However, if the diarrhea is severe, lasts for more than a few days or the stool is accompanied by blood or mucus (even if it is not soft), take the cat to your veterinarian immediately.

## Hairballs

Hairballs (balls of hair that are ingested during grooming, then later vomited) can be a problem for all cats, but plague longhaired cats most frequently. If your cat is vomiting a lot of hairballs, more frequent brushing and a commercial hairball remedy such as Petromalt can help.

Make sure the hairballs come up and that your cat is eating, drinking, and defecating properly. A hairball can cause severe problems if it gets caught in a cat's intestines. See your veterinarian for more severe cases, or if the cat is vomiting more than just hair.

## Allergies

So far I have not heard of a cat who is allergic to other cats, but cats do develop allergies to both external and inhaled allergens. Allergic cats may display many different symptoms, depending on the cat and the allergen.

Flea allergy dermatitis is one of the most common allergies in cats. Signs include excessive scratching, biting, hair loss (particularly on the back and stomach), and red, pimplelike lesions. The chemicals in flea collars can also cause an allergic reaction. If your cat loses the hair and develops redness under his flea collar, remove the collar immediately.

Cats can also be allergic to certain particles in the air, such as plant pollens, house dust, and other inhalants. These kinds of allergies may be inherited. Signs include paw licking, sneezing, redness, and scratching. The signs are about the same as those of flea allergy dermatitis, but no fleas are present.

Your veterinarian may do tests to determine the cause of the allergy. Cortisone injections are usually given to treat an allergy.

Cats may also develop allergies toward certain foods. If you notice that a certain brand of food is causing itchy skin on your cat, cut that food out of your cat's diet and try something else.

Many cats have what is called food intolerance and will develop loose stool with flecks of blood. Intestinal parasites must be ruled out, and then your veterinarian should recommend a special diet.

Some cats develop an allergic chin rash or lip ulcers in reaction to plastic feeding bowls. Many veterinarians recommend using crockery or china feeding bowls.

## Internal Parasites

Although indoor cats are far less likely to get internal parasites, they still can. Intestinal parasites are spread primarily by fecal-oral contact (ingesting eggs or larvae in some way, such as by licking another cat's anal area), and if you bring a new cat into the home, you could unknowingly be bringing parasites in with him. Some intestinal parasites can be obtained from killing and eating rodents (roundworms) or by ingesting insects (tapeworms), and even indoor cats can, on occasion, get hold of these pests.

Keeping your environment clean and using good sanitary practices with the litter boxes will help eliminate parasitic infections.

All intestinal parasites are diagnosed primarily through stool samples checked by your veterinarian. These checks should be done regularly, whether your cat seems sick or not, because there is a period of time after the cat is infected (the prepatent period) when he won't show clinical signs.

Commercial, over-the-counter dewormers are not recommended, because they may or may not be intended for the particular parasite your cat has. Let your veterinarian choose the specific medicine that's best for treating your cat.

Following are some of the parasites that may cause problems for your pet.

### Roundworms

Roundworms, one of the most common intestinal parasites to plague kittens and cats, are spaghetti-like worms that are contracted primarily either prenatally (in the uterus) or by eating rodents. Signs of roundworms in kittens include thinness with a potbelly, a dull coat, vomiting, coughing, and diarrhea. In the case of a severe infestation, the cat may vomit the worms. Adult cats may show no signs yet still be infected with the parasite. Two or more treatments may be necessary to kill all the parasites in your cat's system.

### Tapeworms

Tapeworms are contracted primarily by ingesting infected insects, such as fleas, or may be spread by eating rodents or raw meat. The dried segments of the worms (and sometimes the live ones) can be seen on the anal area of the cat, and they resemble grains of rice. Other signs of tapeworms include weight loss and occasional diarrhea.

```
A Healthcare Tip

Have all new cats tested for worms and disease before bringing
them into your home, especially if you have other cats. If need be,
keep the new cats in isolation until the results of all the tests are
back, and until they have been dewormed.
```

Keeping your cat free of fleas and making sure he does not eat wild
rodents or raw meat will help prevent tapeworms.

### Hookworms

Hookworms generally infect cats when the cat swallows them or their
eggs. They may also penetrate a cat's skin or be contracted prenatally.
Indoor cats have an advantage if you keep their environment clean.
Make sure all potted plants or indoor gardens use sterilized potting
soil. Signs of hookworm infestation include diarrhea (often bloody),
anemia, and weakness. Two or more treatments may be necessary to
rid kitty of these dangerous parasites.

### Coccidia

Coccidia is an intestinal infection caused by a protozoa, and is commonly found in kittens. Adult cats tend to build up an immunity to
coccidia. Coccidia produces bloody diarrhea that may or may not be
tinged with mucus. Medication is usually sulfa drugs, and good san-
itation is important. It is also necessary to sterilize the environment
after a coccidia infestation has been detected.

### Heartworms

When people think of heartworms, they usually think of dogs, but
heartworms can infect cats as well. Transmitted by mosquitoes, it's
rare for indoor cats to become infected by heartworms, unless an
infected mosquito gets into the house and bites the cat.

Heartworm larvae migrate through the animal's body and grow to maturity in the chambers of the heart. Signs of heartworm infection include weight loss, coughing, anemia, swollen abdomen and legs, vomiting, and heart and liver damage, followed eventually by death. However, if caught early, injections of thiacetarsamide will kill the adult worms in the heart. As long as all goes well, another dose will be administered two months later to kill the microfilaria left behind in the animal's bloodstream.

If you are concerned about heartworm in your cat, a blood test, followed by preventive treatment, can help put you at ease.

## External Parasites

Many nasty creatures, such as fleas, ticks, mites, and ringworm, can attach themselves to our indoor friends. Knowing what to look for, what to do, and how to prevent infestations will keep these little buggers in check.

### Fleas

Fleas can cause many problems for cats, including dermatitis, tapeworms and, in extreme cases, anemic reactions that may even lead to death. Small kittens, especially, should be kept flea-free. Heavy flea infestations have been known to cause high mortality rates in catteries, especially in the case of newborn kittens.

The best defense against fleas is prevention. These pesky little bloodsuckers love to breed and hide in carpeting, upholstery, cracks in wood floors, and along walls, using your beloved companion (and you) as a hop-on meal.

At one time, battling fleas was one of the toughest challenges a pet owner faced. But today there are flea preventives that work unbelievably well and are safe for your cats, you, and the environment. Make sure you read all the labels and apply the products exactly as recommended, and that you check to make sure they are safe for kittens.

Frontline is one of the most common flea preventives on the market today. It kills both fleas and ticks, and only needs to be applied once a month. Frontline also offers a spray. Simply spritz it onto your

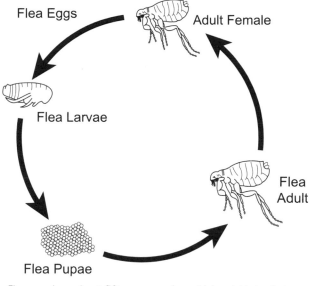

*Fleas produce about fifty eggs per day, which quickly leads to an infestation.*

cat, and it will provide an effective flea and tick control for cats or kittens. The active ingredient is immediately distributed over your cat's body and begins to kill fleas shortly after application.

Program, a tablet you give to your cat, works by interfering with the flea's breeding process. Thus, the number of fleas gradually diminishes, provided there are no animals coming in and out of the house carrying new fleas in with them. If your only pets are indoor cats with no exposure to other animals that may bring fleas into the house, Program is fine. It does not kill ticks.

Advantage is applied in the same way as Frontline. The liquid is placed on the back of the cat's neck and kills any fleas that come into contact with the cat.

At only a small cost per month, these methods are definitely less expensive than the old exterminators, flea bombs, and dips, and are much less traumatic for the cat and much safer for the environment. If you live in an area where fleas are a serious problem, it will be to your advantage to keep your cats indoors and to use the best flea preventative possible.

---

**✎ Online Resources**

Many new flea medications have recently appeared on the market, including inexpensive and generic brands. Some others you might want to look into include Adams Flea and Tick Mist, Capstar, and Bio Spot for Cats. If you want to learn more about flea products and see a good comparison chart, visit:

www.1800petmeds.com

---

Which product you choose will depend on your preference, budget, number of cats, and whether you have animals who go in and out of the house. The products can be bought online, in pet supply stores, or through your veterinarian. When buying flea-control products, ask your veterinarian for the safest and most effective brands to use on your cat. Flea shampoos and collars are available as well if that is the route you prefer. Don't mix flea products unless instructed to do so by your veterinarian (such as using Frontline in combination with a flea collar).

## Ticks

Ticks can transmit many diseases to your cat and to you, including Lyme disease and Rocky Mountain spotted fever. If you find a tick on your cat, remove it immediately using a pair of tweezers. Grasp the tick near its head and pull out firmly and carefully. It may take a few seconds to remove the tick. Be sure you haven't left the tick's head embedded in the cat's skin, as this can cause a serious infection.

After the tick is removed, dab a little antibiotic ointment on the spot. A lump may appear in that spot. This is normal, but watch the area for redness or irritation. Dispose of a tick very carefully. Never crush them between your fingers, because that exposes you to any disease they carry. The best method is to put them in a jar with a little alcohol, and then seal the jar tightly.

Check your cat for ticks when doing your home health exam. Pay special attention to ear flaps, head, neck, shoulders, and feet. Ticks vary greatly in size, depending on the species and how long they have been on your cat. The most common ticks range from small, flat bugs (the size of a small dot) to approximately one inch around when they are engorged. The ticks that carry Lyme disease are very tiny and are barely visible without magnification, even when engorged, so do check carefully.

Though it's rare for indoor cats to get ticks, they can be brought in on you or on another animal. For this reason, I use Frontline, a common flea preventative that also kills ticks, for my dogs and sometimes the cats (in case the dogs carry a tick in on their fur).

## Ringworm

Despite its name, ringworm is not a parasite but a fungal infection of the skin that is highly contagious among cats and to humans. Circular, hairless lesions with a red outer edge, flaky skin, and hair that pulls out easily are all signs of ringworm.

Ringworm organisms last in the environment for a long time. Cats will eventually clear the organism on their own (in weeks or months), but can still transmit the fungus to people and other pets. The treatment is an oral medicine (fulvicin) prescribed by your veterinarian or a lime-sulfur dip and antifungal ointment. For lesions on humans (circular or semicircular itchy areas, generally on the forearms and neck), an over-the-counter antifungal cream such as Tinactin should get rid of the problem in a few days.

Once you rid your cat of ringworm, discard or sterilize all cat-related items such as brushes, combs, leashes, and bedding so that reinfection does not occur

## Mites

Ear mites are the most common mites found in cats, and indoor cats are also prone to them (although not to the extent that outdoor cats are). To check your cat for ear mites, look into his ears with a flashlight. Dirty-looking ears, scratching at his ears, tilting his head, and keeping his ears in a horizontal position are all signs that the cat may have ear mites.

Your veterinarian can give you prescription drops to put in the cat's ears and instruct you on how to administer the medicine and how often. Some cat owners think ear mites are not serious and do not need to be treated. That is absolutely not true. Ear mites are very painful for your cat, and the sound of the mites moving about in the ear canals is also very disturbing for the cat. Ear mites need to be taken seriously and treated immediately.

Besides ear mites, there are also white mites, chiggers, maggots, and lice. White mites resemble large particles of dandruff and can cause extreme itching. Flea sprays may be effective in helping to eliminate these, but in severe cases see your veterinarian.

A small orange or red mite attached to your pet's belly, ears, head, or legs may be a chigger. If you remove one of these pests from your cat, watch the area closely for infection. For heavy infestations, ask your veterinarian for the proper insecticide.

Sometimes lice are hard to spot, as they are very tiny. Severe itching may be a sign that these microscopic pests are present. Lice are rare on cats, but they can occur. Your veterinarian can make the proper diagnosis and give you a shampoo that will eliminate them.

## More Serious Ailments

While indoor cats are generally safe, there is no way to protect them from all illnesses all the time. Environmental and genetic factors can still combine to make your cat ill. You cannot treat any of these problems yourself, but you can recognize them early on and get your cat to the veterinarian promptly.

### Asthma

Sebastian is a cat living every day with severe asthma. It is terrible to hear him coughing, wheezing, and having trouble breathing—the symptoms of asthma. There is no cure, but steroids such as prednisone (administered by a vet) can help.

### FLUTD

Once called feline urologic syndrome, or FUS, this complex array of urinary tract diseases—which includes bladder stones, urethral blockage, and urinary tract infection—is now collectively called feline lower urinary tract disease (FLUTD). The signs vary depending on what is actually the problem, but can include bloody urine, straining to urinate or urinating very often, avoiding the litter box, or crying out while straining. If you see any of the signs, get your cat to the vet immediately. Such symptoms could mean a blockage, particularly in males, which could be deadly if it is not treated right away.

## Kidney Disease

Usually this problem is seen in older cats, but younger cats can develop it, too. Generally referred to as renal failure, it means that the cat's kidneys are no longer functioning as they should be. Many cats will stop eating and/or will drink more at the onset. If you see an increase in the amount of water your cat drinks and increased trips to the litter box, bring him to a vet right away. A blood test will determine kidney function. If the test results are poor, your cat might need extensive IV fluids, which require a few days in the hospital to get the kidneys functioning again. Often, you will have to follow up with subcutaneous fluids at home (see page 183).

## Heart Disease

The signs of heart disease in cats vary depending on the cat and the type and severity of the disease. Some cats can live with heart disease as long as it is discovered early and the proper medications are prescribed. Heart disease can also kill quickly. One day the cat may seem fine, the next he is gasping for breath. Sometimes sudden deaths have been linked to heart disease. Watch for difficulty breathing, any weakness in the legs, coughing, or abdominal swelling.

## Upper Respiratory Infections

Cats can't catch colds from humans and we can't catch a cold from a cat, but cats do get their own feline upper respiratory infections. Sneezing is usually noticed first, so if your cat begins sneezing, particularly if there is a runny nose and/or discharge from the eyes, he might have a cold. Let your veterinarian take a look. Antibiotics might be prescribed. Upper respiratory infections weaken the immune system and can open your cat up to other infections.

## Seizures

Seizures in cats can be caused by many factors. They are most common in cats with kidney disease, but can also be caused by many other factors such as trauma, brain injury, tumors, and epilepsy. If your cat has a seizure (which can be mild or severe—from a stiffening of the body to complete tremors, drooling, and urinating), do not attempt to move him unless he is in danger of falling or injuring himself. Generally, seizures only last a few seconds to a minute or two at most.

A cat in a seizure has no control over his bodily functions and is not aware he is having one. Once the seizure has ended, the cat will be disoriented, weak, and shaky. Pet him, talk soothingly to him, hold him if you wish at this point, but wait until he is coming back to himself before bringing him to the vet. Seizures are not painful and by themselves are not fatal (though the disease or problem that caused the seizures might be, so have your cat checked right away).

For a seizure accompanied by a high temperature (over 104ºF), place ice packs around the cat's inner thighs and under his front legs. If a seizure lasts longer than five minutes, or if the cat goes in and out of seizures for several hours, take the cat to your veterinarian or an emergency veterinary hospital immediately. An injection of phenobarbital or Valium may be necessary to stop the seizures, or there may be a more severe problem. Phenobarbital is usually the medication prescribed for a cat with ongoing seizures.

## Diabetes

As obesity becomes a more prevalent problem in cats, so does diabetes. An overweight cat is more prone to developing the disease, but there may also be a genetic predisposition. Usually a cat with diabetes will stop eating and become lethargic. The cat may become very thirsty and urinate more frequently.

A blood sugar test will need to be done at the vet hospital. If your cat needs insulin shots, your vet will show you how to administer them. Be sure the shots are given exactly as the vet instructs you. Oral medications, which work well for diabetic people, have so far not proven effective in treating cats. If the diabetes is minor, the vet may simply prescribe a special diet for your cat.

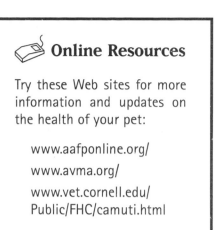

**Online Resources**

Try these Web sites for more information and updates on the health of your pet:

www.aafponline.org/
www.avma.org/
www.vet.cornell.edu/
Public/FHC/camuti.html

## Caring for a Sick Cat

Home care for ill cats is becoming more and more popular. The reason might be due to rising vet bills or the fact that indoor cats are a more integral part of the family. And what better place for a cat to recover than in the familiar territory of their own home? Cats, like people, seem to do better recovering from an illness at home, where familiar surroundings and caretakers mean more attention and less stress.

If your cat is injured or ill but is able to come home, he will require special care and a lot of love from you. A sick cat should be placed in a separate room away from noise, household traffic, and other animals. Make him a bed that is warm, soft, clean, and washable. You can use a lined cardboard box or the cat's regular bed—just make sure the sides are low enough for him to get in and out easily, taking into consideration his particular illness or injury. A litter box and food and water dishes should be set up near the cat's bed for easy access. Your veterinarian can recommend the best foods and feeding schedules.

Keep your sick cat warm and dry at all times. Remove any soiled bedding immediately and replace it with fresh bedding. Keep any medications your cat will require nearby (but safe from accidental ingestion by the cat), and be sure you know the proper methods and doses your cat will need. Never give your cat aspirin or any other type of human medication for any reason, as these may be toxic. Consult your veterinarian before giving any medications.

You know your cat best. However, follow your veterinarian's advice on any health or emergency situation.

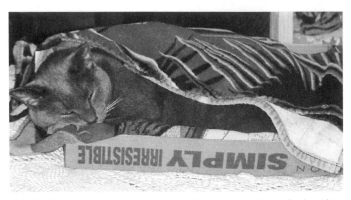

*An ill cat should be kept warm and comfortable, and in a quiet location.*

## Administering Medicine

Giving medicine to a cat can be a harrowing experience for both you and the cat if you do not know how to do it properly. The first step in avoiding disaster is to ask your veterinarian to show you how to properly administer the medication, and pay close attention to how it is done.

When you are ready to give medication to your cat, it is best to have someone help you to restrain him. If this is not possible, wrap the cat from the neck down in a large towel. Make sure the towel is tight enough so the cat can't get his front legs up and out, but not so tight that you choke him.

Hold the cat with one hand, and administer the medicine with the other. You can place the cat on a counter or on your lap—whichever is easiest on you and calmer for the cat. I prefer to set my cats in my lap while at the same time holding the cat's legs between my own.

### Tablets

The most common medication you may have to administer is a pill. Every cat reacts differently to taking a pill. Some pills have a flavor that cats find appetizing. If this is the case, the cat may eat them on his own with no help from you. But most pills just taste like medi-cine, and, for obvious reasons, most cats despise having their mouth forced open and a pill shoved down their throat. In these situations, effective restraint and quick action are important.

Hold the cat against your body or have an assistant hold him for you. Place your hand over the cat's head, palm down, enclosing the head. Gently place your thumb and forefinger on the back corner of each side of the cat's mouth. Tilt the cat's head back carefully and apply gentle pressure to the sides of his mouth. With your other hand holding the pill, gently push down on the cat's jaw and open his mouth. Place the pill at the back of the cat's tongue as far as you can. Then gently place your hand around the cat's mouth while you close it, to prevent him from spitting out the pill. Stroke his throat to aid in swallowing. You can also blow a small, quick puff of air at the cat's nostrils—this stimulates a swallowing reflex. Slowly release your hand from his mouth. If the cat licks his lips, the pill has been swallowed.

Watch your cat carefully when you release him, just in case he's managed to fool you by hiding the pill deep in his mouth. If he has, he'll quickly spit it out and you can try again. Feeding your cat a small treat while he's still in your lap may help to ensure that he swallows his medicine—but first check with your vet, because some medications cannot be given with any food.

Some pills can be crushed up and hidden in the cat's food (get your veterinarian's okay on this before doing it), but usually if a pill is placed in whole, the food will be devoured and only the pill will remain. If you're giving medication this way, you must supervise while the cat eats to make sure all the medication is given and no other animals get it.

### Liquids

Liquid medicines can be given several ways. Some can be mixed with food, others can be administered with an eyedropper or syringe (without the needle). Ask your veterinarian which is best for the type of medicine prescribed and the exact dosage to administer.

If you're using a dropper or syringe, place one hand over the cat's head. With your forefinger, lift the side of the cat's cheek. Carefully insert the syringe or dropper into the cat's mouth and dispense the liquid slowly, giving the cat time to swallow. Be sure to rinse the syringe or dropper after each use.

*Injections*

At one time, it was unheard of for a person (other than a serious cat breeder) to give injections at home. But now it is becoming common practice. Diabetic cats need injections up to three times per day. A cat with kidney disease might need intravenous fluids administered subcutaneously (under the skin) daily for the rest of the animal's life. This practice has given many cats a much longer life span. My beautiful polydactyl cat, Candy, lived to be 20 years old after being diagnosed with renal kidney failure at age 17. Administering lactated ringers (one type of IV fluid) each day gave her an extra three years of good health.

If you must give injections to your cat at home, make sure your veterinarian shows you the proper way to do it. If you have any questions or problems, don't hesitate to call your veterinarian and ask him or her what you need to know.

Make sure you keep all the equipment clean, and don't leave needles around on the counter for your cat(s) to find.

*Skin Creams and Ointments*

Creams and ointments may be necessary to treat cuts, bites, or abscesses, or to prevent infection around sutures. It is important to follow your veterinarian's recommended schedule when applying these, and to be sure the cat does not lick them off. Your veterinarian may recommend what's known as an Elizabethan collar—a large, round piece of material that fits around the cat's neck and prevents him from licking his body or scratching his head. These collars are certainly not comfortable for a cat, so be gentle and patient if your cat needs one, and give him lots of extra love. An alternative that is less annoying for the cat is to spray a bit of bandage with a taste deterrent such as Bitter Apple and then tie it over the affected area.

*Eye Ointments and Drops*

To administer any eye medication, start by washing your hands. Then gently hold the cat's head still with one hand. Your forefinger should be just above the cat's eye and your thumb below. Pull the eye open

## Subcutaneous Fluid Tips

Few people like needles, and cats don't care for them, either. Giving fluids to your cat can be a smooth or a traumatic experience, depending on the cat's personality, your patience, and the kind of experience you make it for him.

First, make sure the needle is positioned correctly. If not, you could have a slow flow and the cat will get impatient. You can also try feeding him and talking softly or giving him treats to make this a pleasant experience.

Make sure you really lift that skin and form a good pocket before poking the needle in, and be careful it doesn't go all the way through. Just a tiny bit in should do it. Watch the drip. If it seems slow, move the needle a tad (not in or out, but side to side). Sometimes you might be hitting a small bit of skin or tissue that blocks the needle from letting out enough fluids. If the needle is not in a "pocket" under the skin it will take longer because you will have a slow drip.

When I gave fluids to Candy, I always made sure the drip was almost a pouring spout or a very fast drip. Up at the top, near the base of the bag where the fluid comes out, you should be able to see the speed of the drip. If you can't, then the tube reservoir is too full and you need to turn the bag upside down without a needle on and with the scroll knob open all the way, so air will force the fluid back into the bag. Then, put the needle back on and close the knob so the fluid is trapped. Turn the bag back and there should be NO fluid in that small tube that sticks out of the bottom of the bag. Remove the needle cap and open up the knob. Let the fluid spill out the needle into a sink and watch the flow in the reservoir. When all the air is out of the tube, close it and recap the needle.

*Never* use a needle more than once. After just one use needles become dull and painful for the cat. Also, bacteria forms on the needle once it's used, so you would risk a bad infection. A smaller needle causes less pain (I used 25 gauge). Try not to poke the same place all the time.

very gently, but not too forcefully. With your other hand, squeeze the prescribed amount of ointment into the eye, being careful not to touch the tip of the tube to the cat's eye. Close the cat's eye and hold for only a few seconds, allowing the ointment to penetrate the eye.

For eye drops, carefully wipe off the area around the cat's eye with a clean swab. Hold the cat's head as for ointment, and apply the prescribed number of drops in each eye. Then gently hold the cat's eye closed for a couple of seconds.

### Ear Drops

Hold the cat's head firmly, gently grasping the outer ear. Fold the outer ear back carefully and apply the drops directly into the ear canal (do not stick anything down into the ear canal, since this can do damage). Then gently massage the base of the ear.

These are just some of the medicines your veterinarian may prescribe, depending upon the nature of your cat's injury or illness. Make sure you follow his or her instructions carefully, and don't hesitate to ask questions. Getting it right is vital to your cat's health and well-being.

## Household Emergencies

Emergencies can and do happen, and it is a good idea to know what to do to ensure minimal suffering and maximum recovery for your cat, just in case. Even if no physical injuries are apparent, it's a smart idea to get your cat to a vet as soon as possible after an emergency, such as a fall. Internal injuries are invisible, and can prove fatal. A veterinarian should look at even something as minor as a small cut, just in case an infection has set in. Here are some signs to watch out for:

- Shock (pale or white gums, rapid heartbeat, rapid breathing, confusion, low temperature)
- Cold ears
- Hot, sweaty foot pads or ears

- Different-size pupils
- Pupils not responding to light
- Fever
- Respiratory distress
- Seizures

## Be Prepared

Emergencies, by definition, come upon you all at once. The first thing you need to do is remain calm. You will not help the cat or yourself by panicking. It's much easier to keep your cool if you've done some preparation. Here's what you can do in advance to be ready for emergencies:

- Have a veterinarian who knows your cat. This way, any allergies to medicines or other health conditions will already be on record when the cat arrives at the hospital.
- Keep a list of emergency numbers near your phone, including your regular veterinarian and an emergency animal clinic, in case your regular veterinary hospital does not have emergency hours.
- Keep an emergency first-aid kit on hand for your cats.

In an emergency, do what you can to stabilize the cat, then seek professional help. Look carefully at the cat and the situation, so you can figure out what has happened and communicate that calmly and clearly to the veterinarian. By evaluating the cat and knowing what is wrong, you can help your veterinarian determine the best way to help your cat recover.

## Approaching an Injured Cat

If the cat is conscious, approach him carefully. Cats may lash out in fear when they are injured, no matter how friendly they are normally. Move slowly and do not rush forward. Bend down to the cat's level slowly and speak in a soothing tone. Reach your hand slowly toward

## Your Emergency First-Aid Kit

You probably have a first-aid kit at home or in the car for your family. Now you need one for your cat. Using a box with a hinged lid, fill it with the following:

- Blunt-edged scissors
- Blunt-edged tweezers
- Tick remover (tweezers can be used, but commercial tick removers are available through your vet or pet supply shop)
- Gauze bandages
- Wrap-around bandage (preferably the self-adhesive type made for pets)
- Cotton balls
- Hydrogen peroxide
- Rectal thermometer
- Milk of magnesia*
- Petroleum jelly
- Immodium A-D*

*Use these items only under the advice and direction of a veterinarian.

the cat. If he shows no sign of aggression, get him to the veterinarian as soon as possible, talking to him and reassuring him all the way (see the section "Moving an Injured Cat" later in this chapter).

If, however, the cat lashes out at you, you will have to take steps to restrain him. A blanket, pillowcase, towel, or piece of clothing placed over the cat's head (allow room for breathing) is your best bet. Hold the animal firmly by the back of his neck. An injured cat may be difficult to work with, so get help if at all possible.

### Checking Pulse, Respiration, and Temperature

Check for vital signs, particularly if the cat is unconscious. First check to see if he is breathing, then check his heart rate if you can. To check your cat's pulse, press your forefinger and middle finger against the inside of his inner thigh, near the groin. You can count the beats for 60 seconds or count for 15 seconds and multiply by four. The heart rate should be approximately 140 to 240 beats per minute.

Watch your cat as he breathes, and count either the inhalations or exhalations, but not both. Again, count for 60 seconds or for 15 seconds and multiply by four. In a healthy cat, the respiration should be 20 to 30 breaths per minute.

If the cat is bleeding, control the bleeding as best you can (see the sections "Bandaging" and "Tourniquet") and get the cat to the veterinarian right away. If not, you may want to check his temperature. To do this, have someone hold the cat, if possible, or wrap the animal in a towel or other restraint that allows for free breathing. Using a rectal thermometer (the human kind is fine) lubricated with petroleum jelly, insert the thermometer into the cat's anus. Use gentle pressure until the thermometer is inserted about one inch. Hold the thermometer gently in place for two minutes. Digital thermometers are also available. The temperature should be 100.4 to 102.5°F.

## Artificial Respiration

For a cat who has stopped breathing but still has a heartbeat, start artificial respiration. Place the cat on his side and open his mouth to check for any obstructions in the throat. Clean the cat's mouth of any blood or mucus.

With the cat's mouth closed, place your entire mouth over his muzzle and exhale gently until you see his chest expand. Remove your mouth from the cat's until you see his chest deflate. Continue this while transporting to the veterinarian or until the cat is breathing on his own.

Never practice artificial respiration or heart massage on a healthy cat; you could injure him.

## CPR

CPR (cardiopulmonary resuscitation) is required if the cat is not breathing and has no pulse. This is a life-threatening situation, and CPR should be done immediately and continuously. For CPR to be effective, you must combine artificial respiration with heart massage. CPR will not be effective, however, if there is extensive external or internal bleeding.

Place the cat on his right side. Clear away any blood or mucus in his mouth and begin artificial respiration, as described in the previous section.

But you must also perform heart massage. There are two ways this can be done. One method is to place your entire hand around the cat's chest so that his breastbone is resting in the palm of your hand. Your thumb and forefingers should be in the middle of the cat's chest. Another method, particularly if you have small hands or the cat is large, is to place the heel of one hand on the left side of the cat's chest, just behind the elbow. Place your other hand on top of that hand.

With either method, compress the chest for a count of two and release for a count of one. Continue this with the artificial respiration (five chest compressions followed by one breath, and so on) while transporting the cat to the veterinarian or until the cat's heartbeat is regular and he is breathing on his own.

## Moving an Injured Cat

Be careful when moving an injured cat, whether he's unconscious or not. Injuries can be aggravated in transport.

Move an unconscious cat carefully away from any dangerous area using a coat or blanket supported underneath the cat. If you can get help, have someone else hold one end of the coat or blanket, or have them restrain the cat during the move. Be careful the cat does not slip from the blanket or coat. If a box or other secure container is available, gently place the cat inside for ease of transport.

If the cat is conscious and struggling, be careful. An injured cat may lash out. Speak in soothing tones and move slowly. Wrap the cat in a blanket or towel, making sure his paws are restrained but being careful not to aggravate any wounds. You can hold the scruff of the neck and support the legs to help subdue him. The cat should be placed in a carrier or box that closes securely and transported to a veterinarian immediately.

## Shock

After an injury, a cat may exhibit signs of shock: pale or white gums, rapid heartbeat, rapid breathing, confusion, low temperature. Check the cat's airway to be sure he is breathing normally. Check for and remove any foreign substances blocking the airway. Check for a heartbeat (perform CPR if necessary) and control any bleeding.

Keep the cat warm with a blanket or coat and roll up a towel or piece of clothing and place it beneath his hindquarters to keep them elevated. As with all emergencies, transport him immediately to the veterinarian.

## Electrical Shock

The first step is to get the cat away from the source of the shock. Do not touch an electrical cord or a cat who is being shocked; unplug the cord or move it away from the cat with a wooden object, such as a broom handle. Then feel behind the left front elbow for a heartbeat and check for breathing.

If the cat is breathing, transport him to a veterinarian immediately. If the cat is not breathing but there is a heartbeat, perform artificial respiration and transport to a veterinarian (simultaneously, if possible).

If the cat is not breathing and there is no heartbeat, perform CPR as you transport the cat to the veterinarian (if possible).

## Poisons

Not every poison is swallowed. Some poisons enter through the skin or through open wounds. Others can enter the lungs through inhalation. Signs of poisoning vary but may include vomiting, convulsions, coughing, abdominal pain, diarrhea, and delirium.

If your cat comes into contact with a poisonous substance, seek veterinary help as soon as possible. If you know what the poison was, take a sample with you and, if your cat is vomiting, take a sample of that, too.

With some swallowed poisons, inducing vomiting using hydrogen peroxide (one teaspoon every 10 minutes), followed by a few teaspoons of activated charcoal (available through your veterinarian), can help. Get the cat to the veterinarian as soon as possible. However, if the poison is a petroleum-based compound or a strong acid or alkali, do not attempt to induce vomiting. Your local poison control center can give you more information on the recommended action to take. For more information, you can also contact the Animal Poison Control Center toll free at (888) 426-4435. Or you can visit its Web site; go to www .aspca.org, then select "Animal Poison Control Center."

## Wounds

If your cat gets a small wound, carefully clip the hairs around the area with a pair of blunt-edged scissors and wash the wound with soap and water. Then dab with hydrogen peroxide or Betadine and an antibiotic ointment to kill bacteria. Do this at least three times a day, making sure the wound stays free from dirt and foreign particles. Look for any signs of swelling or redness, which suggest an infection.

If the wound is extensive or if bleeding can't be stopped, stitches may be necessary and veterinary care is required. A rash or skin infection should be treated by a veterinarian, because oral antibiotics may be needed.

## Bandaging

Bandaging a wound may help keep the bleeding under control until you get to the veterinarian. To bandage a limb or tail, wrap gauze firmly (but not too tightly) over the wound. Place a strip of adhesive tape at the end of the bandage, then wrap the tape securely over the bandage in overlapping bands. Bandage the entire limb and be sure the tape overlaps some hairs, to avoid slipping.

When bandaging a wound on the body, chest, or abdomen, first place a piece of clean gauze over the wound. Take a large, rectangular piece of cloth and cut one-inch strips on either side, about a third of the way into each side. Place the cloth so the uncut part fits securely around the cat's belly. Tie the strips over the cat's back. Transport the cat to the veterinarian immediately.

## Tourniquet

If the cat is bleeding and direct pressure does not stop it, applying a tourniquet may help. Do not place a tourniquet over a joint or fracture. Any strip of cloth can be used as a tourniquet. Do not use rope, wire, or string.

Place the cloth about one to two inches above the wound. Tie a loose loop around the limb. Lay a strong stick or a sturdy pencil over the tie, and tie another loop on top of it. Twist the stick until the bleeding has ceased (no tighter). You must periodically release the tourniquet and then retwist it as you quickly transport the cat to a veterinarian.

## Splint

In the case of a break or fracture, applying a splint will help keep the bones immobile until you are able to get kitty to a veterinarian. The splint should be a long, rigid, flat piece of material—in a pinch, a rolled-up magazine will do. If the cat is in extreme pain or fights when you try to apply the splint, stop, wrap the break in a sturdy towel, and transport him to a veterinarian immediately.

If the cat does not fight, place the splint over the fractured area, making sure the joints directly above and below the break are included. Tape or tie the splint securely, but not too tightly. You don't want to cut off the circulation. Transport the cat to a veterinarian immediately.

## Object in the Eye

Flush the eye with clean water or saline immediately. If a chemical was splashed into the eye, wrap a clean gauze pad around the eye to cover and protect it. If there is bleeding, apply gentle pressure to the area until the bleeding has subsided, then wrap the eye. Transport the cat to the veterinarian.

## Burns

For second- or third-degree burns, place cold packs on the area of the burn and transport the cat to the veterinarian immediately. Do not apply ointments.

For mild burns, place ice packs on the affected area. Leave in place for at least 15 minutes. Cover the area with clean gauze and watch it carefully for signs of infection. If the cat seems to be in pain, take him to the veterinarian. An examination will rule out any problem, and pain-control medication may be required.

## Smoke Inhalation

Remove the cat to an area where there is plenty of fresh air. Check the cat's breathing. Use artificial respiration or CPR if needed, treat for shock, and seek veterinary care immediately. Carbon monoxide poisoning should be treated in the same manner.

## Choking

Signs include pawing at the mouth, pale tongue, distress, and unconsciousness. Clear the cat's airway by placing your hand over the cat's head and gently pushing your thumb and forefinger on either side of the cat's mouth just behind the long canine teeth. Tilt the cat's head back carefully. If you can see the object, try to remove it with your fingers or tweezers. Do not attempt to remove a needle or other sharp object. Take the cat to the veterinarian immediately.

If you cannot remove the object, lay the cat on his side and place your palms behind the last rib on both sides of the abdomen. Press your palms together in a thrusting motion several times, firmly but carefully. If the object still does not dislodge, transport the cat to the veterinarian immediately.

If your cat has swallowed a string or thread and it is hanging from the animal's mouth or anus, pull gently to remove it. However, *do not pull if you meet with any resistance.* Transport the cat to the veterinarian. If you suspect your cat has swallowed a string, even if he shows no signs of distress, a trip to the vet is in order.

## Go to the Vet!

None of the advice in the preceding section is intended as a cure-all. It is only as a way of stabilizing the cat to optimize his chances of survival. Always transport an injured cat to a licensed veterinarian as soon as possible.

# Natural Disasters

In February 1986, a flood-weakened dam threatened to destroy Marysville, California. Many people were evacuated from their homes with little notice. In October 1990, fire swept through Southern California, destroying homes and killing many humans and animals. On August 23, 1992, Hurricane Andrew devastated parts of Dade County, Florida. More than 100,000 cats and dogs were left homeless. In March 1993, a blizzard struck the Northeast and left behind lost lives and homes without power. On January 17, 1994, a major earthquake shook sleepers from their beds in Southern California.

Regardless of where you live, a natural disaster is a real threat to you and your pets. Whether your area is susceptible to a tornado, hurricane, blizzard, earthquake, fire, flood, or mudslide, you should not only prepare yourself, but also know how to protect your cats.

## Before Disaster Strikes

Prepare yourself. The Red Cross provides a pamphlet on disaster preparedness that offers information on what you can do for yourself in case of an emergency. Follow its advice on storing food, blankets, water, flashlights, and medical supplies. After you've prepared a disaster kit for yourself and know what you will need to do, you can then prepare a disaster kit for your cat (see the box on page 194). To contact the Red Cross, visit its Web site at www.redcross.org, write American Red Cross National Headquarters, 2025 E Street, NW, Washington, DC 20006, or phone (202) 303-4498. For disaster assistance information, call (866) GET-INFO (866-438-4636).

The following steps will help you prepare for a disaster. Then, if the worst happens, at least you'll be ready.

1. Devise a plan before disaster strikes so you will know what to do and will be organized in the event of a quick evacuation. Your cat should be trained to enter a cat carrier without fuss (see chapter 2).

2. Know your cat's favorite sleeping and hiding spots. If you are warned of an impending disaster and need to evacuate, you will not want to waste precious moments searching for the cat(s).

3.  Keep your cat's vaccinations up to date. In a stressful situation, a cat's immune system is weakened. And if the cat is brought to a shelter, he may come into contact with bacteria that could cause disease.

4.  Know in advance where you can go with your pet(s). Most evacuation shelters are for humans only and will not allow you to bring your cats with you. During a natural disaster, humane societies and animal shelters are usually overburdened, so finding alternate arrangements is essential. Maybe a friend in another area can help. If you are lucky enough to find a shelter that will allow you to keep your cat(s) with you, be sure you have an ample supply of food, water, litter, and cleaning supplies. Do not remove your cat(s) from the carrier while in the shelter unless it is essential, always use a secure harness and leash and do not allow cats to roam.

5.  If you must leave your cat(s) behind, make sure they have an ample supply of dry food and water in nonspill dishes. Set the cat(s) up in a room away from windows or breakable objects.

---

### Your Cat's Disaster Kit

- Medical supplies, such as gauze, ointments, and bandages
- Special medications, if your cat takes them
- Newspapers and towels
- Leash and harness (one set for each cat)
- Clear photographs and descriptions of each cat
- Nonspill food and water dishes
- Litter box and litter
- Plastic bags
- Enough cat carriers or cages to hold all your cats
- A week's supply of water and dry cat food

*Don't leave your cat inside a closed building if you need to evacuate during an emergency.*

The bathroom may be the safest room in the house. Keep cats, dogs, and other pets separated, if possible. Fights can occur in traumatic situations, even among animals who are friends. Cats should have access to someplace high in the event of a flood.

6. In some disasters, such as earthquakes, there will be no warning or time to evacuate. Having carriers and food supplies ready and knowing where to find your cat(s) can prevent some problems. Make sure your cats are always wearing identification, preferably with your phone number and the number of an out-of-state friend. If your cat gets out of the house and becomes lost, you will want a number on the animal's tag that can be reached in the event your phones are out for days at a time.

## The Aftermath

Once the disaster is over, many cats will be extremely frightened and will hide for days or weeks. Aftershocks from earthquakes can last for a long time and may cause some cats to continue hiding. It is essential that you keep the cat calm as best as you can. Pet, talk to, and reassure the cat often, but do not force him from his haven (unless it is a dangerous area). Make sure the cat has food, water, and a litter box available.

If you come home after an evacuation and find your home damaged or destroyed, arrange to have your cat(s) stay with a friend or relative until you are resettled. If you are fortunate enough that your home was spared from disaster, do what you can, if possible, to help others who were not quite so fortunate. Organize a neighborhood search for missing pets, or offer to volunteer at your local shelter or humane society. Teach public awareness about what to do before and after a disaster. Help others to keep their pets as safe as you want your cats to be.

# 9

# The Lost Cat

Quite a few years ago, my cat Taffy, an indoor cat all her life, slipped out a door that got stuck open accidentally. I, along with a posse of friends, searched frantically for her, to no avail. I was distraught as to where she could have gone, and my mind constantly relayed unwanted images of what could have happened to her. She was, after all, an indoor cat and unaccustomed to life outdoors. I could not sleep that night and, in my insomnia, frequently ventured into the kitchen to stare out the window.

At 2:30 A.M. on the second night of Taffy's disappearance, I was gazing out the window and there she was—at the door waiting to be let in, as if she did this every day. I brought her in, where she was warmly welcomed by family members, and afterward I settled into bed with her under the covers, snuggled up against my body. I will never know what she did, where she went, or what her experiences were during the two days she was gone. She never again attempted to escape, but she still wanted to go outside, sometimes waiting by the door and staring at it as if it would magically open, before giving up.

## What to Do

Most cats raised indoors show little desire, aside from a slight curiosity, to experience what is on the opposite side of that door, particularly if a cat is trained from the start that the door to the outside is off-limits to her and a no-no. But even indoor-only cats can get out. A door inadvertently left open too long or a ripped screen can provide access for a curious cat's escape. An indoor cat who gets out, particularly a cat who has never been outdoors, could easily get lost because she is not as familiar with the terrain as an outdoor cat.

With prevention and care you will spend many long and happy years with your companion and not have the worry and pain of a lost cat. However, if your cat does get out, there are steps you can to help ensure her safe return.

### Don't Panic

Stop and think: How long has the cat been missing? Knowing your cat, where would she go? Are there wooded areas the cat may have gone into or a busy street nearby? Ask your neighbors if they have seen your cat. Walk the streets and woods calling your cat. Get help from others, if possible. Use something that makes a sound your cat is familiar with and comes to, such as a can opener or a squeaky toy. This may or may not help, depending on the cat, but it won't hurt to try.

When Taffy disappeared, my friends and I searched the woods behind my house, which is where Taffy was last seen heading (a neighbor remembered seeing her because she "had never seen that cat in the neighborhood before").

If there is an abandoned building in the area, you might want to look there, or ask the police to look around (don't roam around inside abandoned buildings by yourself, as they might be dangerous). Check trees, parks, restaurants, garbage dumps, and construction sites. Leave your name and phone number with everyone you come in contact with. Bring flashlights, even in daylight, for looking in dark corners and crevices.

## Contact the Authorities

Call the police to report your cat missing. In larger communities the police will probably tell you to contact an animal shelter, and you should do this as well. Also contact pounds, pet shops, and veterinary hospitals. Leave your name, phone number, and a description of your cat with them.

If your cat is gone for more than a day, keep in contact with animal shelters, police, fire departments, pet supply shops, and veterinarians.

## Make Posters

You will also want to make up posters at this point—which is why you should always keep a good-quality, clear photograph of your cat available in case you need it. Make one poster and copy it. You will want to distribute the posters as widely as possible, so make plenty—around one or two hundred posters. Many office supply stores or quick-copy shops can print up that many copies quickly and inexpensively.

Your poster should have the following information:

- LOST CAT and REWARD should be printed in large, dark letters at the top. People tend to be more helpful if there is a monetary reward involved. However, you should omit the amount of the reward, to prevent extortion.

- A sharp, clear photograph of the cat should be placed in the middle.

- A detailed description of the cat—breed, color, size, and any distinguishing markings—should be put under the photo. Put these in words that someone unfamiliar with cats will understand.

- Your phone number(s) should be dark and legible and placed at the bottom of the poster. The phone number of a friend who agrees to be a contact can also be helpful.

*Don't* put your cat's name on the poster, or any sentence like "Answers to the name of . . ." (most cats in a strange situation will not respond to their name, anyway). Also, don't put on the poster clues

**LOST CAT**

Lost February 18, 2004
Domestic Shorthair,
Black and white with "goatee"

Has only three legs
Is an indoor cat

**REWARD**

If found please call:

(phone numbers, including cell #)

about the cat's behavior, where she was lost (the cat may have been picked up and dropped off somewhere far away), the gender (someone unfamiliar with cats may not know the difference between a female and a neutered male), and whether or not she was wearing a collar (the collar may have slipped off or been removed).

Place the posters everywhere the cat may have gone, as well as all around neighboring towns and as far as you can around your area. Place them on telephone poles, in grooming salons and store windows, and at colleges or universities, schools, pet supply shops, veterinary hospitals, shelters or pounds, and police and fire stations. Give copies to everyone you come in contact with, including the letter carrier, newspaper carriers, and delivery persons.

If your cat is missing for more than a few days, check the posters regularly and change them as needed, just in case they are torn off or rained on.

### Place an Ad

Place an ad in the "Lost and Found" section of local newspapers (particularly daily papers) and on the Internet. Check the ads for "Found Cats," too; someone may have found your cat and placed an ad. You also might want to try Internet lost-animal sites, such as disc.server .com/Indices/61236.html. Call radio and television stations that offer advertising or public announcements. The more people you reach, the better.

If there is a pet detective in your area and you can afford it, you might want to hire him or her to help search for your missing cat.

## What Not to Do

- Don't respond to any lost-pet callers alone. Go with a friend and meet somewhere safe.

- Don't invite a caller to your home.

- Don't fall for money scams. Remember, you can offer a reward if your cat is found, but don't specify an amount.

- Don't give out all the information about your pet. If someone calls and says they have your cat, ask them a question about the cat's appearance that was not revealed on the posters or in any information you gave out.

- Don't give up! Remember, there have been cases of cats who have disappeared for weeks, months, or even years, then came home on their own or were found. If, by some unfortunate fate, your cat never returns to you, know that at least you did all you could.

## Preventing Escapes

The first step in preventing escapes is to teach your cats that the door is off-limits. Chapter 2 explains how to accomplish this. The following techniques can also help prevent your cat from getting lost.

Check screens regularly, including those on doors, to make sure they fit tightly and are not torn. Make sure doors close properly. My cat Taffy got out because the screen door stuck open when it wasn't pushed closed.

Tell anyone who comes into your home that you have indoor cats, and ask them to close doors securely when they enter and exit. Make sure screens are placed securely in all open windows.

When you have workers or delivery people in the house, don't rely on them to watch out for the cat. Put her in a safe room and keep the door closed—no matter how much she complains.

## Identification

Keeping identification on your cat will prevent someone from thinking she is a stray and keeping her, and may help the cat be returned

*A lost cat can get disoriented and wander away from the home. Place things with familiar smells around the outside of your home.*

to you if she is found. There are three forms of ID available for cats: collar and tag, tattoo, and microchip. The collar and tag is the most common.

## That Clinking Sound

A collar and tag with your name and phone number (not your address) can be kept on your cat at all times, if you choose, even though the cat lives indoors. Medical information and the fact that your cat is an indoor pet should also be on the tag.

Many types of tags are available, including metal ones or inexpensive, plastic reflective tags. They can be purchased at any pet supply store.

The collar should be a breakaway or expandable type, so if it gets caught on something the cat can pull it off and will not be strangled. The collar should fit on your cat just loose enough that you can slip two fingers beneath it. Do not put tags on a flea collar, as they are not constructed for this purpose.

You may wish to keep only one tag on your cat's collar. Cats have very sensitive hearing, and two or more tags constantly clinking together can drive a cat nuts.

Acclimate your cat to wearing a collar when she is young, if possible. Some cats, if they are not accustomed to a collar, may practically kill themselves trying to get one off. They may get a paw or their jaw caught in the collar, and this can have serious consequences.

The disadvantage of collars and tags is that they may fall off or can easily be removed. They can also pose safety problems. If you live in a situation where your indoor cat cannot possibly escape, a collar is probably not necessary.

## Tattoos

Tattoos can be placed on the inner thigh or inside the cat's ear. Most people choose the inside of the ear, because a tattoo on the inner thigh is not noticeable unless the area is kept shaved. The exception, however, is show cats. Many cat registries forbid show cats to have a tattoo inside the ear.

The number you use for the tattoo is your choice, the most common being your Social Security number, a number chosen number by the tattoo registry, or the cat's registration number (in the case of pedigreed cats). Whatever number you choose, it must be registered with a national tattoo registry or the finder will have no way of contacting you, even if your cat's tattoo is discovered.

Usually a collar and tag with the tattoo registry phone number is also worn to alert people to the presence of a tattoo. But if the cat loses her collar and the tattoo is on the inner thigh and not shaved or readily noticeable, the shelter or pound picking up the cat may not know to look for a tattoo.

## Collar Safety

A cat in my neighborhood, apparently lost for a long time (possibly an indoor cat who had escaped and lost her way), was attacked by a dog. In the bustle of getting the cat to the vet, I did not notice that she was wearing a brown, unbreakable flea collar that was snaked around her neck and down under one front leg. She had apparently slipped a front leg through and was never able to get any further.

Unfortunately, the cat did not survive the attack, and the reason for her inability to escape became obvious when the vet and I saw the collar. The area around the collar was raw, bald, and festering. That cat had been suffering a long time.

Expandable collars, too, can sometimes get caught around a cat's legs or in her mouth. I've seen cats with cut lips and broken jaws from collars caught in their mouths. Breakaway collars are a bit better, but it is vital with any collar to make sure it fits properly so that the cat cannot get a paw or jaw up under the collar. Unfortunately, flea collars generally don't have tight-enough buckles to maintain the right fit, and will sometimes expand after lengthy use.

In my opinion, tattoos and microchips are far better identification than a collar. If you must use a collar on your cat, err on the side of caution and check the fit carefully and regularly. Do not leave flea collars on for more than a month, and always use the safest collar available.

Tattoos are a reliable form of identification. However, they can fade with time and may have to be redone. Tattooing can be done by your cat's veterinarian, breeder, or groomer, or at a tattoo clinic. Often towns or clubs will hold a tattoo clinic for people who wish to have their pets tattooed. For more information, contact Tattoo-A-Pet at (800) 828-8667 or I.D. Pet at (800) 243-9147. Or visit www.tattoo-a-pet.com.

 **Online Resources**

If you want more information on finding lost pets, this site has a wealth of information, including a lost pet poster generator:

www.lostpetfoundpet.com

## Microchip Technology

A microchip is a tiny computer chip, about the size of a grain of rice, with a registered number. It is injected into the cat, usually between the shoulder blades. This is a permanent form of ID that cannot be lost or altered.

The microchip implant has been around for quite some time now, but was not a popular method of identification until recently. That's because most veterinarians and shelters did not have the scanning device needed to detect a microchip, but now many do. Some communities that require cats to be registered are now giving the owner the choice of a microchip implant for their cats.

Like a tattoo, a microchip must be registered with a national registry. For more information about microchips, you can visit www.homeagainid.com or contact AVID at (800) 434-2843, or see www.avidid.com. The American Kennel Club also operates a microchip registration and recovery service that is open to all types of pets. You can contact the AKC Companion Animal Recovery at (800) 252-7894, or visit www.akccar.org.

# 10

# Cats in the Kitchen

The small cat was feeling weak. He could hardly lift himself up anymore. It had been a long time since he had seen his humans. The wooded area where he was lost was interminable. Every now and then he was able to catch a mouse or a mole to eat, but these animals did not taste as good as his cat food and certainly didn't make him feel any stronger. He doubted he would even be able to catch them now. One day, he came across some garbage left behind by campers and ate the food left there—just some stale bread and one half-eaten hot dog. It wasn't until weeks later that he was found by a kindly old man. He brought the cat into his home and fed him some milk. It tasted good, but made the cat's tummy feel a bit queasy. The man looked at the tags on the cat's collar and made a phone call.

The cat fell asleep in the sunshine on a cozy carpet, and when he awoke, his people were there, lifting him into their arms and showering him with love. He would once again eat the foods he loved and grow strong. He would again be happy.

## Good Feline Nutrition

Like the little kitty in this story, your cat is a domestic animal and relies on you to feed him the foods that will keep him strong and healthy. A 100-percent nutritionally complete diet of the proper food can help prevent problems such as obesity, nutritional deficiencies, finicky eating, and plant chewing, and will help your cat maintain a healthy coat and a stronger immune system.

**Online Resources**

For more on the foods you feed, visit AAFCO—the Association of American Feed Control Officials—at:

www.aafco.org

Cats enjoy a variety of foods, including vegetables. Feeding your cat greens such as cat grass and lettuce is fine, and even healthful, but remember that cats are true carnivores. Only meat provides the amino acid taurine, plus other essential nutrients cats need to survive.

You should choose a diet that suits your cat. For instance, kittens require a higher protein diet to grow strong and healthy. A cat with a kidney disease or some other illness might require a special diet lower in proteins and other nutrients to avoid making the condition worse. Make sure you know what your cat needs and feed him a diet with the right amounts of protein, fats, vitamins, minerals, and carbohydrates.

Cats should be fed a varied diet and not strictly fish, lean meat, or liver, as these products alone will not be completely balanced and will cause deficiencies.

## Canned Food or Dry?

When dry or canned food is fed in the correct amounts based on your cat's age and size, either should meet kitty's nutritional requirements. Dry food is good for a cat's teeth, so it is a good idea to feed dry food either regularly or as the cat's staple diet. Dry cat foods have more caloric density, which means there is less water in half a cup of dry food than there is in the same amount of canned food. However, cats also benefit from the high water content of canned foods. Most cats enjoy eating a combination of dry food and canned.

A kitten 8 weeks to 4 months of age should eat three to four meals a day of a high-quality kitten food (canned and/or dry). Starting at about 1 year of age, two meals a day is fine.

How much you feed your cat at each meal will depend on the cat and the type of food you feed. Several factors should be considered:

- Is your cat overweight?
- Does your cat require a special diet? (If so, follow your veterinarian's recommendation.)
- Are you feeding a high-calorie food?
- Does your cat pick little bits all day long or gorge himself at every meal?

Dry food can be left out for your cats as long as they do not overeat and are not on a special diet. The food should not be allowed to spoil or get stale if the cat does not eat it. I leave dry food out for my cats, and the turnover is so quick that it does not have a chance to get stale. I also feed a quarter can of moist cat food (six-ounce cans) to each cat twice a day; there are no leftovers, but if there were, I would not leave them around for more than about 15 minutes. My cats eat only what they want and do not gorge themselves. However, this is not true for all cats. If your cats eat more than the recommended amount, I would advise feeding two square meals

 **Online Resources**

The best way to know exactly what you are feeding your cat is to read the labels. That's where you will find the best information, as well as ingredients, guaranteed analysis, feeding instructions, and nutritional adequacy. An excellent Web site outlining how to read the labels on your kitty's food is:

www.petplace.com/
articles/artShow
.asp?artID=3502

a day and removing any leftovers as soon as the cats walk away from their dishes.

It's a good idea to monitor your cat's weight over time. If, as an adult, his weight remains the same, continue to feed what you are feeding. However, if the cat seems to gain or lose weight, you can feed more or less until the cat's weight is steady.

## Feeding Time

If you have more than one cat and they get specific meals during the day, they should be able to enjoy their meals quietly and without hassle. Feed each cat in a separate food dish away from traffic and noise. Some of my cats eat quickly and search out food from the slower cat's dishes. To prevent this, watch the cats as they eat to make sure the slower cats are allowed to finish their food. Feeding slower eaters in a different room can also be helpful.

Cats should be fed away from strong odors such as litter boxes and chemicals. It's not fair to them, and they can develop finicky eating habits. Don't forget how sensitive their noses are!

*Feeding your cat up high will help him feel more secure while he eats.*

Feed your cats in a quiet area that is not going to make them fear their dishes and feeding time. Cats like to be up high, so if you can, place your cat's dish up on a cat tree and let him eat there, rather than feeding him on the floor,

If your cat develops bumps under his chin, a bit like acne, he might have an allergy to his dish. Sounds strange, I know. But if you feed your cat in a plastic dish, that may be where the problem lies. Cat food should be served in ceramic or stainless steel dishes. Ceramic and stainless steel are also less porous, and therefore trap less bacteria. Food dishes should be flat-bottomed with low sides and should be washed thoroughly after each meal.

## Water

You must provide your cat with fresh water at *all* times. The water should be changed at least twice a day to keep bacteria from building up in the dish, particularly in hot weather.

If your cat eats canned food as a large part of his diet, he'll get water in his food and may drink less from his water dish. However, you must still leave fresh, clean water available for your cat at all times.

Some cats prefer to drink from a running water source. When my cats Taffy and Candy were in their final stages of kidney failure, they drank a lot of water. I bought them a Drinkwell Pet Fountain. This and other types of pet water fountains are available at pet supply stores and on the Internet. The Drinkwell Fountain offers a separate reservoir so the water lasts a long time. This fountain also provides a carbon

**Online Resources**

For more on feline water fountains, try:

www.petsmart.com/
www.tjspetshop.com/
search.php/keywords=
drinkwell/src=goo/
kws=drinkwell
www.petcarecentral.com/
drinpetfoun.html
www.radiofence.com/
drinkwell_pet_fountains
.htm

*Drinking fountains are a fantastic source of fresh water.*

filter so water is always clean and fresh. Just put in the filter, fill the unit with water (I use spring water), and plug it in. Every now and then, the flow valve will get clogged with debris and cat hair (as your cat drinks, hair sometimes falls into the water). But the unit is easy to take apart, clean, and put back together.

Cats sometimes like to drink from the toilet bowl, because the water is renewed often and is cold. While this is generally not recommended (cats can fall in and become trapped in the cold water), just in case your cat sneaks a sip while you're brushing your teeth, don't use toilet bowl cleaners that release chemicals with every flush. And make sure you rinse the bowl thoroughly every time you clean it.

## Do Cats Need Milk?

Milk is not a necessary part of your cat's diet and may cause upset tummy and diarrhea. There is no reason to feed your cat milk. Almost all pet supply stores (especially the chain stores, such as PetSmart and Petco) sell "cat milk," a special drink that contains lactose-free nonfat milk. Usually taurine and other essentials are added, as well. It comes in a variety of flavors and several brands. Many cats love it, others don't. Read the instructions and make sure to refrigerate it after opening the container.

# Obesity

In today's health-conscious society, almost everyone is concerned about calories and losing weight. Yet we continue to overindulge our felines until their sides bulge, and it's just as unhealthy for them as it is for us.

Obesity is the most common nutritional disease in cats today. It is estimated that 12 percent of all house cats are overweight, with females having the highest incidence. Obesity can contribute to heart trouble, respiratory difficulty, stress, low heat tolerance, diabetes, arthritis, and a lowered resistance to illnesses. Obese cats can also have trouble bathing themselves and may let their grooming habits slide. Obese cats tend to die much younger than cats of proper weight. The average life span of an obese cat is 6 to 12 years old, compared with a 15- to 20-year life span for an indoor cat of ideal weight.

A cat who is approximately 15 to 25 percent over his ideal body weight is usually considered obese. To tell if your cat is overweight, place your hands on either side of his rib cage. If you cannot feel your cat's ribs through his fur, the animal is overweight.

Obesity is not caused by neutering a cat or by keeping your cat indoors. Obesity in cats is caused by the same thing as it is in humans: eating more calories than are needed to sustain one's activity level.

Many people allow their cat to eat anything he wants. They get tired of the cat's incessant meowing and begging for food, so they give in. This can be a fatal mistake.

Although many cats are nibblers and only pick a little bit all day long, some will practically inhale their food as if it were their last meal. You must know your cat's eating habits to know how and when to feed. Some cats can have food in their dishes all day and will regulate themselves. Others

*Obesity can cause many health problems. It's far better for your cat to keep him trim and fit.*

must be fed a set amount at a specific time or they will overeat. It's a myth that all cats know when to stop eating and can regulate their own weight. Some can, but others eat too much out of boredom or

 **Online Resources**

Some cat food companies today make foods specifically designed for the indoor-only cat. For more information and analysis of this food, visit:

www.feline-nutrition.com/indoor.htm

simply because they like their food, and will become obese. Obesity is dangerous to a cat's health, so you must regulate the food intake of these cats.

An obese cat should be thoroughly examined by a veterinarian to rule out the possibility of thyroid disease. Follow the veterinarian's recommendations on diet and exercise.

### Dieting Tips for Cats

- Provide your cat with plenty of toys and scheduled playtimes.
- Three or four small, measured meals a day are preferable to one large meal.
- Treats should be restricted to a small handful of dry food that would normally be a part of the cat's regular meal.
- Don't feed your cat table scraps.
- A high-fiber, low-fat, low-calorie food should be fed to a cat who needs to shed weight. Food should be changed over gradually by mixing a little more diet food with the regular food each day until the cat is eating all diet food. The high-fiber food will make your cat feel full, enabling you to feed less.

If your cat is on a diet, don't expect immediate results. Cutting back on food intake will decrease your cat's metabolic rate, therefore causing him to burn fewer calories, so be patient.

## Finicky Eaters

Does it seem that no matter what you feed your cat, he turns his nose up and walks away? Your cat is finicky. Many well-meaning owners allow their cats to become finicky eaters by removing a food the cat will not eat and endlessly offering something else, or only feeding one favorite food all the time.

Finicky eating is not harmful in itself, as long as the cat is eating a nutritionally complete cat food. However, you should try to prevent finicky behavior because someday your cat may need to switch foods because a specific brand is no longer available or the cat needs a special diet.

With a finicky eater, leave food out for only ten or fifteen minutes at a time, then remove it whether or not the cat has eaten. This will give your cat the message, "Either you eat or you go hungry." However, never let your cat go more than twenty-four hours without food.

Try mixing small amounts of a different food with your cat's favorite food, each day adding more and more of the other food. Do this with different flavors and varieties.

Do not allow food to go stale. Most cats like fresh food and may turn their noses up at food that has been sitting out.

Being finicky should not be confused with a nibbler or a cat refusing to eat due to illness. If your cat refuses to eat even his favorite foods after several days, it is time for a trip to the veterinarian. Any refusal to eat, even for a day, accompanied by vomiting, diarrhea, listlessness, panting, or lethargy is the sign of a medical problem—go straight to the vet.

Often stress will cause a cat to go off his food. If this seems to be the case, you will have to find the cause of the stress as soon as possible to get your cat eating again (see chapter 3 for more on stress). The weather may affect your cat's food intake, as well. Although outdoor cats are more affected than indoor cats by changes in weather and seasons, an indoor cat, too, may show small differences in his eating habits due to seasonal changes.

Before dubbing your cat finicky, check the following to be sure something else is not the cause:

- Food dishes. Some cats won't eat out of deep dishes or dishes that are dirty. Use shallow dishes and keep them clean.

- Have you recently changed foods? If your cat is not accustomed to a different food, try making the change gradually.

- Is your cat on any medications? Some medicines may dull your cat's appetite or make certain foods taste different, causing the cat to avoid them.

- Canned food that is cold from the refrigerator may not be palatable to some cats. Warm the food to room temperature before feeding.

## Treats and People Food

Feeding your cat treats and people food is fine, as long as they do not add up to more than about 10 percent of your cat's daily food intake. More than that and you will throw your cat's complete and balanced diet out of balance. Do not feed your cat raw meat, poultry, or fish, as they can contain parasites, toxoplasmosis, or salmonella. Cook any meats thoroughly and remove all bones before giving the meat to your cat. Never feed a cat anything with caffeine and never feed him chocolate. Not only are these things unhealthy, they can be lethal to a cat.

Your cats will love a pot of fresh lawn grass, grown inside just for them. Cats in the wild enjoy an occasional grass salad, and your indoor cat will, too. Growing grass for your cat has the added advantage that it will help keep kitty away from your houseplants. Pet supply stores carry kits with seeds and a small container in which to grow the grass. You can also feed small amounts of lettuce and other vegetables if your cat will eat them, but not as a staple diet. Cats require greens to aid in digestion and to pass hairballs, but they cannot digest them in large quantities.

## Vitamin and Mineral Supplements

As long as you feed your cat a diet that is complete for cats (as stated on the label), there is no need to feed additional vitamins or minerals. Your cat will get enough of these in his diet, and extra supplements can throw a diet out of balance.

### Homemade Treats

Ever thought of making your cat some treats yourself, rather than buying premade treats from a store? Try this recipe.*

**Cat Cookies**
*Makes 18 treats*

> 1/4 cup warm water
> 5 tablespoons Parmesan cheese
> 3 tablespoons soft margarine
> 1 tablespoon cod liver oil
> 1 cup white flour
> 1/4 cup soy flour

Directions: Preheat oven to 300°F. Combine water, cheese, margarine, and oil. Add flour and form a dough. Roll to 1/4 inch thick and cut with a cookie cutter (how about some animal shapes, just for fun?). Bake on an ungreased cookie sheet for 20 to 25 minutes, or until cookies are lightly golden. Cool and store in the refrigerator.

*These treats are for occasional consumption only and shouldn't be fed as a staple diet. If your cat has food allergies or special dietary requirements, check with your veterinarian before making them.

There are certain situations, however (such as metabolic difficulties, pregnant cats, and young kittens), where a vitamin or mineral supplement may be needed. They should be given only under the advice of a veterinarian.

## Strange Eating Habits

Some cats develop the habit of sucking, chewing, or even eating odd things, such as socks or blankets. It's not known exactly why some cats do this, and each cat's reason is most likely different. It may be a redirected suckling behavior—a leftover feeling of comfort from the days of suckling on Mamma. Or maybe the cat needs something in

her diet that she's not getting. The cause could also be stress or an eating disorder—similar to the way a person might overindulge when he or he is stressed.

If your cat has this rather odd habit, as my cat Taffy did (she would suck and chew blankets, which for her was a form of suckling), don't worry. Usually it causes no difficulties. But be careful—watch that your cat does not ingest anything that contains hazardous chemicals. Also, stringy materials can cause blockages and problems within the intestinal tract.

If the problem gets out of hand, keep the preferred material out of your cat's reach and contact your veterinarian. Interestingly, more scheduled playtime has been shown to be effective in many cases of compulsive chewing.

# 11

# The Aging Cat

As my cat Candy aged, she became less active, grew thinner, and drank more water. She was diagnosed with renal failure at age 17. She died at age 20.

At one time it was unusual for a cat—even an indoor cat—to live past the age of 13 or 14. But now, with modern medicine, better nutrition, the indoor lifestyle, better information available through the Internet, and easier access to understanding and solving problems, it is not uncommon to see a cat who is 18 or 20 years old or even older.

Part of your responsibility when you acquired that cute little kitten is seeing her through her geriatric years. You changed with your cat, grew with your cat, shared happiness and tears with your cat. Now it's time to share in her old age and provide her with extra care during these delicate years.

The old adage that one year of a cat's life is equivalent to seven years of a human's is a misconception. If that were true, a 1-year-old cat would be the equivalent of a 7-year-old child. But a cat is psychologically and sexually mature at one year of age, while a 7-year-old child is not; a cat experiences much more development in her first two years than a human does in the first fourteen. After the first two years, though, a cat's life proceeds more slowly in relation to the

*Precious is almost 18 years old and is still going strong.*

life of a human, and each feline year equals approximately four human years. The general consensus is that at about age 7 a cat can be considered "middle-aged," and age 14 and beyond is "old."

## Geriatric Changes

As your cat ages, certain psychological and physiological changes occur: cloudy eyes, diminished hearing, graying fur, less luxuriant coat, flabby muscles, senility, stiffness, arthritis, and decreased activity are all common. Many of these changes are the natural and inevitable consequences of aging, but there is much you can do to make your cat more comfortable. And some of these changes are the results of diseases that become more common as a cat ages. That's why cats over the age of 10 years should have yearly geriatric screenings.

Eyesight may begin to fail, due to glaucoma, cataracts, or macular degeneration. These problems can be treated. Cats may also lose their eyesight. They usually adjust quite well to blindness, but there are steps you must take to ensure the cat's safety. Sharp objects should be removed, and access to high places should be secured or blocked off. Do not move things around; a blind cat will become familiar with the placement of things and may become confused if things are placed differently. My blind cat, Teisha, gets around fine as long as everything is kept in the same place, but the moment something is moved she becomes disoriented. Before touching or handling a blind cat, let her know you're coming by speaking softly to her as you approach.

Older cats may lose their hearing, and you may notice a lack of normal responses because of this. Be sure to announce your approach to a hearing-impaired cat by touching the cat gently or letting the cat see you coming.

Older cats may develop problems with their bowels that can cause constipation, diarrhea, or incontinence. If any of these problems occur, take your cat to the veterinarian immediately. Metabolism changes may also cause the cat to eat more or less than before. Often older cats

## Cat Years vs. Human Years

| Cat's Age | Human's Age |
|-----------|-------------|
| 6 months | 10 years |
| 8 months | 13 years |
| 1 year | 15 years |
| 2 years | 24 years |
| 4 years | 32 years |
| 6 years | 40 years |
| 8 years | 48 years |
| 10 years | 56 years |
| 12 years | 64 years |
| 14 years | 72 years |
| 16 years | 80 years |
| 18 years | 88 years |
| 20 years | 96 years |
| 21 years | 100 years |

will lose weight, although their appetite may not change. This is normal, but it is important to watch for signs of excessive weight loss, which can indicate a medical problem. Your older cat may become thin if she does not get enough protein in her diet.

Obesity should also be a concern for the owner of a geriatric cat (see chapter 10 for more on obesity). As a cat's activity level decreases, she may tend to become overweight. This is particularly true for a cat who has always had a tendency to overeat.

An older cat's behavior may also change. Some cats become friendlier with age, snuggling more and always in search of a warm lap to curl up on. Others develop a grouchy attitude and become more easily agitated.

Litter box habits may be affected by age. As a cat grows older, watch for urinary problems. Inactivity, coupled with the inability to hold urine, may contribute to accidents. Problems with mobility, including arthritis, may also make it difficult for your cat to get to her litter box. As your cat grows older, keep her litter box near where she spends most of her time. You may even wish to add another litter box

---

## Senior Treat

The following is a wonderful treat you can make for your geriatric cat that may help encourage her to eat more.

  2/3 cup cooked fish fillet, boned and chopped

  3/4 cup cooked barley

  3 teaspoons steamed carrots, chopped

  3 teaspoons cooked green beans

  2 teaspoons nonfat dried milk

In a bowl, combine the fish and barley. Stir in the carrots and green beans. Place the dried milk in a small bowl. Stir in a little water and pour over the fish mixture. Refrigerate and serve small amounts as treats.

so your cat will not have to go searching for one, thus helping to avoid accidents.

A cat's coat quality and physical appearance may also deteriorate as she ages. Some cats may neglect to groom themselves as often, so it is a good idea to help by keeping up on your cat's grooming. This includes care of the cat's nails. Not scratching regularly could cause an older cat's nails to grow too long.

## Caring for Your Aging Cat

Diet, exercise, grooming, nutrition, love, comfort, and good medical care are all major factors for you to consider as your cat gets on in years. Food intake should be increased or decreased according to the cat's weight (see chapter 10 for more on diet). An older cat's weight may be slightly lower than a younger cat's, but should not be excessively so. Allowing an older cat to become too thin can be dangerous. If your older cat gets sick, she will need a little extra weight to get her through the illness.

An older cat's sense of smell may diminish, causing her to have less interest in food. This could lead to the cat becoming underweight and undernourished, making her more susceptible to disease. A cat food with a stronger aroma may entice her to eat.

But don't overdo it. Obesity can be a health hazard to any cat, but is particularly so with an older one. A cat who is carrying around too much extra weight may live a shorter life than a cat whose weight is under control. Weigh your cat regularly to make sure she is maintaining the proper weight. A good 100-percent nutritionally complete cat food especially made for geriatric cats is ideal for weight control. There are many good brands on the market today. Consult your veterinarian for his or her recommendation.

Keep your cat active with daily play, within the confines of your cat's physical abilities. Cats become less active as they grow older, and you will need to entice and encourage your cat with her favorite toys. If your cat is able and it is not too stressful for her, drag a string up and down the hallway or stairs or roll a ball along the floor so she can give chase. Catnip (for cats who respond to it) is a good pick-me-up for an inactive cat.

An older cat will need much more love and TLC. The geriatric cat may choose to curl up with you on your lap and spend more time being near you. Never be stingy with your attention, as an older cat may appreciate and need it more. If your cat becomes grouchier as she ages, patience on your part is a must. A slower approach may be necessary with an aging cat. As their senses become less sharp, cats become a little less secure emotionally. They need you to understand their slower behavior and give them extra love and attention.

Gum disease is very common with older cats and may affect your older cat's eating habits. Regular dental care is important. Have your cat's teeth checked once or twice a year. You may wish to help by brushing your cat's teeth yourself, if she will allow you to (this is easier if you accustomed your cat to having her mouth touched and opened at a young age; see "The Home Health Exam" in chapter 8). Using a strip of gauze wrapped around your finger, you can rub your cat's teeth with a special cat toothpaste. Don't use human toothpaste because it causes excessive salivation and can create an upset stomach if swallowed.

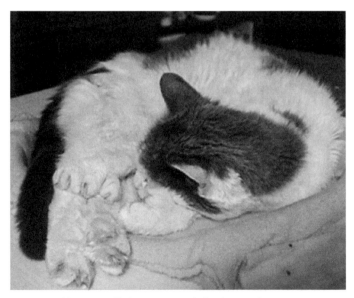

*Your cat will sleep more and play less as she ages.*

The comfort of the aging cat is an important consideration. As their metabolism slows, older cats become more susceptible to disease and are less able to regulate their body temperature. Therefore, it's important to keep your geriatric cat warm. More snuggly beds placed around the house will be welcomed now. On chilly days or nights, keep windows closed so the cat does not get near a draft.

## Health Problems

Regular veterinary exams are a must as your cat gets older. Kidney disease can plague older cats, so watch the cat's normal intake of water and her urinary habits. If your cat seems to be drinking an excessive amount of water, urinating often, or straining, it's time for a trip to the veterinarian. Your cat should also have a checkup if she has any change in litter box habits.

Hyperthyroidism is also common in older cats. If your cat seems to consume more food than normal, urinates more often, and drinks more water, take her to the veterinarian to be checked for an enlarged thyroid gland. Diabetes is also common in older cats. Some symptoms include increased appetite with weight loss, drinking excessive amounts of water, and urinating more frequently.

If you suspect any of these problems, do not hesitate to contact your veterinarian. You will need to keep a close eye on your older cat's health and habits. Keep up with your home health exams (as described in chapter 8) and perform them more frequently. Pay special attention to your cat's teeth. Excessive tartar buildup can lead to gum disease and tooth loss. Also, pay close attention when massaging your cat's body. All lumps should be checked by your veterinarian to be sure they are not cancerous.

Once a year, your older cat should have a geriatric screening done by your veterinarian. This includes urinalysis, a fecal exam, and blood tests. These tests will alert you early to any problems so they can be treated before they become too serious to treat. Cancers of the blood, lymphatic system, and gastrointestinal tract, as well as thyroid problems, are more prevalent in older cats, and regular blood tests can help uncover these problems at early stages.

## Loss and Grieving

There comes the terrible time in all cat owners' lives when they must say good-bye to a cherished feline. Often you are faced with the difficult choice of euthanasia when a cat is seriously ill. It would be selfish to allow a cat to go on living if the animal is in pain and there is nothing more that can be done. This is never an easy decision to make, and it may be difficult to know when the right time is to make it. Talk to your veterinarian, and ask as many questions as you need so you can be sure you thoroughly understand your cat's situation.

If you do make the decision to actively put an end to your cat's suffering, stay with your cat while it is done. It will be hard, but remember: Your cat was a loyal companion to you, and she deserves to have the familiarity of your presence in her last moments.

---

### What If Something Happens to You?

What about providing for your cat(s) if something happens to you? This is a possibility you must think about, because often animals who are not specifically mentioned in a will end up in pounds or shelters.

One option to consider is to leave your cats in a specific person's care. If you know of someone who would be able to care for your cats, then speak with the person and get their permission to name them in your will as the cats' caretaker. You should also designate a sum of money for that person to care for the cats.

If there is no one you know who can care for your cats in the manner you think fitting (including making sure they remain indoors), you may want to find a no-kill cat shelter where your cats will either be adopted (usually no-kill shelters have stricter screening rules) or live their lives in the shelter. Investigate to find a shelter that is clean, to your liking, and has a good reputation.

Make sure you state specifically in your will that your cats are to remain indoor cats and, if you choose to bequeath your cats to a no-kill shelter, it's nice to leave a healthy donation for their benefit.

## Helping Yourself

Letting go is an important step in coping with the loss of a beloved cat. It is normal to feel all the usual signs of depression when a cat dies. Don't be afraid to hurt, and don't let anyone try to minimize your grief.

- Acknowledge the inevitability of your cat's death.
- Hold a ceremony to finalize the event and pay tribute to your cat.
- Allow yourself to mourn freely.
- Seek out family and friends who understand.
- Don't be afraid to talk about it.
- Don't fear or deny your emotions.
- Plant a tree or flower in honor of your pet.

Denial is a natural first stage most people go through when they are grieving. It is difficult to accept the loss of someone so loved. The next stage of grief is generally anger and/or guilt. These are normal, but you should not focus on them. Instead, think of the good times you had with kitty. Do not dwell on your depression.

Plan a burial or a memorial ceremony. Buy a memorial garden plaque (available in some pet supply shops and online) to honor your kitty. There are pet cemeteries around the country, and you may want to consider a service at one near you. Here you can visit kitty whenever you wish and even bring her favorite flowers.

If you find the grief too much to handle, there are support groups where pet owners get together to discuss their losses. It can help to speak to others who have experienced the same pain.

 **Online Resources**

To find memorial stones and plaques, check these sites:

www.oldworldstones.com/

www.rockitcreations.com/
gallery/petmemorials.html

www.exterior-accents.com/
catmest.html

www.kittysites.com/
memorials.html

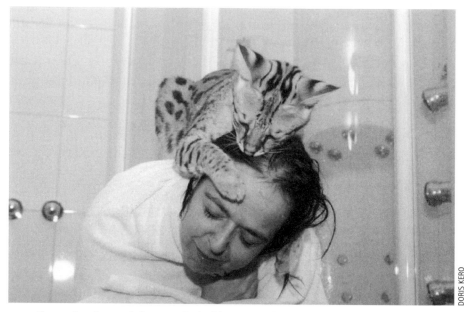

DORIS KERO

*Remember the good times you had with your cat. She lives on forever in your heart.*

 **Online Resources**

There are many sites that offer services to help you cope with loss and grieving:

www.cats.about.com/od/ lossandgrieving/ (articles about loss)

www.almost-heaven.org/ pfp/ (Prayers for Pets)

www.aplb.org/ (Association for Pet Loss and Grieving)

www.avma.org/ careforanimals/ animatedjourneys/ goodbyefriend/ plhotlines.asp (AVMA Grief Counseling)

If you have other pets, do not deny them your love and attention. They will feel the loss as well, so play with them and let them know you still love and care for them. Give yourself time to recover. Do not let your loss deter you from acquiring another companion. You will never be able to replace your cat (nor should you try to), but there are many wonderful cats out there just waiting to share with you all the love and attention you have to give.

# Index